ON CAMERA
AND OFF

LISA THOMAS-LAURY

ON CAMERA
AND OFF

*When the News Is Good
and When It's Not*

CAMINO BOOKS, INC.
Philadelphia

Manufactured in the United States of America

1 2 3 4   21 20 19 18

Library of Congress Control Number: 2017037865

Cataloging-in-Publication data available from the Library of Congress, Washington, DC.

ISBN 978-1-68098-009-7

ISBN 978-1-68098-010-3 (ebook)

Interior design: P. M. Gordon Associates, Inc.

Cover design: Jerilyn Bockorick

This book is available at a special discount on bulk purchases for educational, business, and promotional purposes. For information write:

Publisher
Camino Books, Inc.
P.O. Box 59026
Philadelphia, PA 19102
www.caminobooks.com

I dedicate this book
to my mother, Blossom Howard,
who was with me throughout my journey . . .

I love you, Bebe

. . . and to all those
who suffer with chronic illness.

God bless your stalwart spirits.

CONTENTS

INTRODUCTION

A FAMILIAR FOREBODING overcame me shortly after my plane landed. West Virginia's mountains would be beautiful this time of year. The autumn leaves would be bursting with color. Still, there was an atmosphere of nervous apprehension surrounding me. I had lived most of my life with a constant dread of returning home.

Now I was thinking about the wheelchair and airport attendant that would be waiting for me outside the aircraft, and again I promised myself I wouldn't always need them. I hadn't notified any of my childhood friends about my visit, not having come to grips with them seeing me ill and practically immobile.

Minutes later, my mom met me in baggage claim; the attendant helped load me and my wheelchair in her car, and we headed west from Charleston on Interstate 64, toward West Virginia State University and my hometown of Institute.

When we turned onto Barron Drive just off campus and approached Louise Street, the memories flooded back. Was this the beginning of my devastating health crisis? Was it possible, as some doctors had surmised, that the chemicals from the Union Carbide plant just a few hundred yards from my home—the toxins I had been exposed to growing up—had altered my genes and led to the devastating disease that had struck me so suddenly and brutally two years earlier?

I recalled the mornings my brothers and I walked from our house to our school bus, past the yellow, powder-like substance covering our neighborhood lawns and cars. We knew it wasn't pollen.

CHAPTER ONE

A LITTLE YELLOW
COLORED GIRL

"NOT BAD FOR a little yellow colored girl from Institute, West Virginia," my proud father teased me. He grinned broadly as the play I had written and starred in, "The Girl in the Red Shoes," received thunderous applause from my third- and fourth-grade audience at Institute Elementary.

I was the skinny nine-year-old who, as long as she could remember, had dreamed of becoming a writer. "Shoes" was my premiere literary work, and I loved being center stage in the midst of huge hugs and smiles from my family, my teachers and friends. But it was my dad's words of praise that became fixed in my brain, and it wasn't the last time I'd hear them.

As a reward, Dad gave me my first thesaurus. I spent countless hours turning each precious page and tracing with my fingers the new words I was learning, determined to use them in my future writing.

My name was Lisa Howard, and around this time I met another Lisa Howard. Actually, I didn't meet her, but at lunchtime in my school we were allowed to watch the small television set perched on the shelf above our classroom desks. For the first 15 minutes, while Ms. Howard delivered the midday news on ABC, my sandwich and butterscotch cookies remained untouched. I was transported to a different world. It wasn't only that her diction was impeccably precise, that her voice was immeasurably appealing or that she was the prettiest white woman I had ever seen. She had my name! The show was called *The News Hour with Lisa Howard*. My classmates began prophesying the coming of the new network news anchor!

And I knew then that I *would* pursue a career in communications in some capacity. What I didn't know was that I would rise to unimaginable heights, then fall and rise again for reasons that often had little to do with my talent.

⟋⟍

Institute is an unincorporated community on the Kanawha River near the city of Dunbar. During my childhood, from the 1950s to early 1970s, Institute had a population of about 2,800 people. Nestled in a valley surrounded by mountains, it was known as Chemical Valley because for nearly a century it was home to one of the largest concentrations of chemical plants in the nation. I lived there with my parents and three younger brothers. For my family and other residents, living in Chemical Valley meant recurring industrial accidents that spewed toxic gas emissions, caused explosions in our neighborhood and poisoned the groundwater. It wasn't uncommon to find brown water running from the kitchen faucet or to see the enamel on our bathtubs eaten away. You had to worry about what the same water might do to your skin and teeth.

In 1984, nearly 10 years after I left Institute, Chemical Valley achieved a level of global infamy, if only by association. Thousands of villagers in Bhopal, India, died that year after methyl isocyanate, or MIC, escaped from the Union Carbide plant in Bhopal.

Methyl isocyanate is a chemical used to make pesticides and plastics. The only place in the United States where MIC was manufactured and stockpiled was Union Carbide's plant in Institute. Who knows the long-term damage it may have done to those of us who dwelled there?

⟋⟍

My grandfather built many of the homes in Institute and its surrounding communities from the 1950s to 1980s. He believed that your personal worth was largely determined by what you could do with your hands. He was thrilled that I was a skilled seamstress and made extra money designing and making dresses for women in our neighborhood.

But Papa, who had not finished high school, never commented much on my academic accomplishments. So it surprised me when, years later, local merchants and others in the community told me how elated he was when they congratulated him on my achievements or when he spotted a newspaper article about me tacked on a store wall.

After leaving Institute Elementary, I traveled just 15 minutes away to high school, in adjoining Dunbar, home of the pugnacious Bulldogs. In those days, I studied hard and partied hard, knocking back Bali Hai and Ripple and smoking weed on the weekends. And I was Harvey Chester's girlfriend! First loves can have a powerful influence on 16-year-old girls, but I also had a deep devotion to my schoolwork, so I was enthusiastically hittin' the books and making sure Harvey did as well. Decades later, Harv told me how he appreciated my forcing him to keep up with his studies. My first beau, a bona fide party animal back in the day, graduated from West Virginia State University and became a successful business operations manager at IBM, despite the fact that our high school guidance counselor told him he wasn't college material.

By the time I was a junior in high school, my passion for writing had escalated. I was news and fashion editor of the school newspaper, *The Kennel*, and was planning to attend Marshall University in Huntington, West Virginia.

When graduation approached, I was overjoyed to learn that I would be salutatorian of my graduating class. I had also been awarded a United High School Press scholarship as the most promising high school journalist in the state. On graduation day, my dad took one look at me in my cap and gown and the gold tassel to mark my achievement, and winked. "Like I always say, not bad for a little yellow colored girl from Institute," he said. I beamed with satisfaction.

CHAPTER TWO

TELEVISION
WANTS ME?

In 1972 my journalism scholarship took me 38 miles away from Dunbar, to Marshall University in Huntington, West Virginia. I had visited the campus as part of a special summer program in 1971 and found much of the student body and community still mourning the lives lost in a horrific plane crash a year earlier.

On a rainy hillside in Wayne County, a chartered jet carrying most of Marshall's football team crashed on its approach to Tri-State Airport. It was November 14, 1970. The Thundering Herd was on a return flight from a game at East Carolina University.

Thirty-seven Marshall University football players were aboard the plane, along with the team's coaches, its doctors, the university athletic director and prominent members of the community. All died in one of the worst single air tragedies in NCAA sports history.

Though the university was shadowed by that tragedy, my three and a half years there were a rewarding and productive time that set me firmly on my career path. Majoring in journalism, I was eager at first to become a magazine writer, but those dreams changed during the second semester of my freshman year when an upper-classman friend, Bill Dodson, shared with me a life-altering opportunity. Bill told me that the local NBC television affiliate, WSAZ-TV, Channel 3 in Huntington, was interviewing for a weekend weather forecaster, and he thought I'd be perfect for the job. There were only a few people whose opinions I valued as much as Bill's; his sister, Angie, was among them. She was a Marshall journalism star who became preeminent in her field. She, too, thought I should apply for the weather gig.

THE LURE OF LOCAL TV

In the spring of 1973, I became Huntington's second black weather forecaster. (Years earlier, Adrienne Belafonte, then a student at Marshall and daughter of actor and activist Harry Belafonte, had had a stint as weather girl there.)

I also decided to pledge Angie's sorority, Alpha Kappa Alpha, and this commitment, along with my determination to save some weekend leisure time, didn't always mesh with my broadcasting responsibilities. It wasn't uncommon for me to deliver the Saturday or Sunday evening weather in a colorful head wrap or halter top, having just come from a sorority event, the community pool or my boyfriend's house.

And no one was more supportive of my weekend weather efforts and my sorority antics than my college love, Bobby Harper. As insane as the sorority obligations seemed at the time, I wasn't going to quit. Bobby did everything he could to help me, even hiding me at his apartment on 10th Avenue when necessary.

When spring break arrived, I temporarily avoided the embarrassing hassles of being a pledge by fleeing with Bobby to Fort Lauderdale. It was the first time I'd ever seen the ocean. It confirmed for me something that college life had nearly caused me to forget—that there *would* be life after Marshall.

Bobby and I had met in front of Twin Towers, my dormitory on campus. He had just flown home from Germany after a stint in the Army. I knew we would eventually become an item because of the way he stared at me that night and the way my heart fluttered in response.

He was tall and handsome, with a full beard and dark, sensuous eyes. He and Ms. Allen, his mom, were a godsend during some of my most stressful days. She was like my mom away from home, making sure I always ate well. Her fried chicken and carrot cake were the best I'd ever tasted. Yes, I loved Bobby *and* his mother, and I would realize later just how much I depended on them to make it to graduation.

Eventually my own mother, distressed about my choice of TV attire, decided she could no longer bear to watch my Channel 3 forecasts. But it was because of my unconventional style that I learned my first lesson in the power of TV ratings.

According to station sports chief Tom Jacobs, our Channel 3 news director, Bos (pronounced "Boz") Johnson, was perplexed by my weekend wardrobe and planned to call me in to discuss it. But that was before the monthly ratings showed a spike in viewership. Apparently the size of our nighttime TV audience had grown as more people tuned in to my forecasts, many of them to see what I would wear.

As I approached my senior year at Marshall, I began reporting the news at WSAZ, along with my weather duties. Like some of the other station reporters, I was a one-woman band, shooting my own film for my stories with a 16-mm camera. Much to my delight, my extended report on Huntington's Wastewater Treatment Plant earned me major approval from Bos. He was a widely respected and genuinely nice man who gave me excellent advice in the very early days of my career.

I was thrilled to hear from Bos in the mid-1980s, after I had arrived at WPVI-TV in Philadelphia. When he told me how proud he was of my work and success in the industry, it made all those embarrassing days as a neophyte broadcaster in Huntington well worth it.

Sadly, our TV-3 patriarch died in 2014, after a 53-year career in communications. He spent more than two decades of that time at WSAZ in Huntington. His son, Rob, is now the station's early morning and midday news anchor.

FULL-TIME TV NEWS

After college I had job offers from three television stations across the country: Lexington, Kentucky; Mobile, Alabama; and Oklahoma City, Oklahoma. In my mind at the time, Mobile was as unsophisticated as Institute, and Lexington was too close to home. Oklahoma City was really farther than I wanted to go—more than 800 miles away—but my mom had a second cousin in nearby Norman, so I packed my bags and headed for Oklahoma to begin my first full-time TV job.

At KTVY-TV, the local CBS affiliate, I learned the nuts and bolts of television news reporting and news photography, but I decided I could never make my home there. There were no mountains! I never realized how much I would miss West Virginia's scenic landscape, especially in autumn when it exploded with color. I figured I'd stay a year or so and learn as much as I could.

In those days reporters worked in pairs. I often teamed up with a tall, blond young man named Dave Smith. We shared the use of a CP-16 film camera, much larger than the one I'd used in Huntington. Dave would shoot my story as I interviewed my subject and took notes. Then we'd hop back in our news van and head to the scene of whatever he was covering, and I would return the favor, heaving the nine-pound video camera onto my shoulder to film his report. Back at the station, we would both take our film from the camera and retreat to a small editing room to "splice and glue" the stories that would air on the evening news.

Oklahoma was a new learning ground, and as it turns out, I was there for only eight months before a call came from Nashville, Tennessee.

OPRAH AND ME

Fisk University, Meharry Medical College and Vanderbilt were nearly all I knew about Nashville. My mother had attended Fisk in the late 1940s and had shared many stories about her classmates and the great friendships she had made. Like most people, I had also heard about the Grand Ole Opry, but I had never heard of Oprah Gail Winfrey until the evening before my interview at WTVF-TV.

Decades before she would become an international phenomenon, Oprah Winfrey was a rarity—a young black woman succeeding, even flaunting her talents, in a profession dominated by white men. I sat on the edge of the bed in my hotel room that Sunday night, gazing at the young black woman on the TV screen. She was fabulous! The Oprah we all know today was average-looking then: brown skin, wide-set eyes, thick black hair. Still, she had the most extraordinary presence and voice. Her poise and verbal effectiveness struck me as she anchored Nashville's local Sunday Evening News, solo.

She looked to be about my age, but I couldn't be sure. What was indisputable was how good she was. She was one of the first people I met the next afternoon when I arrived at the station for my interview with news director Chris Clark.

"Well, aren't you a tall drink of water," declared Oprah as I entered the newsroom, escorted by the office secretary.

"Hi," I said. "I'm Lisa. I saw your newscast last night and was really impressed."

We chatted for a while, long enough to learn we were both born in the same year, 1954, which was a historic year for television news; at least four dozen local TV stations opened that year in cities and towns across the country. It was also a banner year for black achievement. The National Negro Network was established in 1954 with 40 charter member radio stations. That same year came the first major league baseball game in which the majority of a team (the Dodgers) was black. And the historic ruling *Brown v. Board of Education* was handed down, the U.S. Supreme Court declaring that state laws establishing separate public schools for black and white students were unconstitutional.

Oprah and I had a lot to talk about. I marveled at how much she had already accomplished, anchoring a weekend nightly newscast in the 29th-largest TV market, and she was equally in awe of the fact that I had filmed and edited my own stories—and that I made most of my own clothes. In later years, after I had been hired as an anchor in Philadelphia and her talk show in Chicago became syndicated, I often visited the Windy City to interview her. She would always tease me, "Hey, Lisa Thomas-Laury, bet you're not still making your clothes with those Butterick patterns."

After my interview with Clark, Oprah invited me to stay overnight at her apartment before my flight back to Oklahoma the next morning. That's when I learned that she was hoping to be hired at a TV station in Baltimore, WJZ, as co-anchor of the nightly news.

We were a pair of chatty 20-somethings that night, talking about everything from new jobs and boyfriends to black history and even the camps we had attended. Both Oprah and I had been nominated in our junior year of high school to attend Girls State, a summer leadership camp sponsored by the American Legion. At Girls State in Tennessee, Oprah had created a piece of artwork that she proudly displayed on her living room coffee table—a replica of a mansion, made of Popsicle sticks.

I managed to land the reporting job at WTVF-TV, but by the time I moved to Nashville, Oprah had already moved to Baltimore and started her new co-anchor gig at WJZ.

Two years later, I learned that she had been turned down for the emerging anchor position that I eventually landed in a bigger market, at WPVI-TV in Philadelphia. I had spent my two years in Nashville mostly reporting. She had the experience as an anchor, both in Nashville and in Baltimore. To anyone on the outside, then, it would have made much more sense to hire Oprah to anchor the noon news in the fourth-largest television market than to risk filling a position like that with a young woman like me who had almost never anchored a newscast, except for brief morning cut-ins in Oklahoma.

To understand the dynamics of the decision in Philadelphia, one has to remember what was happening in television news then. In 1970 the Federal Communications Commission (FCC) had issued a set of regulations prohibiting discrimination against women in broadcasting. There was also a push to hire more minorities in broadcasting. Oprah and I, along with dozens of other African American female journalists, were in high demand because we were double minorities, both women and black.

But there was, as expected, some resistance to change. By 1978, when I was hired in Philadelphia, there was only a handful of young black women and men actually anchoring the news in the larger TV markets like Philadelphia, New York, Chicago, Los Angeles and Dallas. The general managers of some of those stations were cautious about introducing a black person on the afternoon or evening news in cities where a significant percentage of viewers had become comfortable watching white male anchors. And in cities that had the most troubled histories of race relations, like Philadelphia, television stations had to be even more cautious about whom they showcased on their newscasts.

I was well aware that a big part of my appeal to management at WPVI was that I was African American but didn't "look too black." While easing the pressure from the folks at the FCC, I wouldn't "offend" the station's white audience.

There were other TV stations, however, that wanted there to be no uncertainty about the blacks they were finally hiring. In fact, months before accepting the job in Philly, I was convinced that I was passed over for a similar job at WJLA-TV in Washington, DC, the eighth-largest local TV market, because I "wasn't black enough." As one of the WJLA producers later told me, "In this city, if a station is gonna hire a black newscaster, they wanna be sure people know they're black."

Oprah and I would later chuckle about what happened in Philly. We understood the silent message, but we would remain true to ourselves. I wanted a career and a family, and I think Oprah knew even then that she was destined for greatness.

At WPVI, in the fourth-largest TV market, I became one of the most popular and highest-rated local TV anchors in the country. And I would meet my future husband in Philadelphia and start a family. Of course, Oprah moved on to the third-largest local TV market, Chicago, to host her own morning talk show, then beat out the national "King of Talk," Phil Donahue, in the ratings. Later she *owned* her talk show, then her own TV network, and became a worldwide media sensation!

HELLO, PHILADELPHIA

In my early years in Philadelphia, there were some questions about my ethnicity. In the black community, I am sure there was little doubt that I was a "sistah," but I consistently received letters from viewers in Hispanic, Italian and other white neighborhoods, asking if I were of their background.

The truth is that both of my parents were African American, but my blue-eyed mother, Blossom Howard, with her wavy blond hair and extremely fair skin, looked as white as any Caucasian woman. In fact, my mom looked so white that she caused a bit of a kerfuffle at WPVI soon after my arrival.

My mother had driven with me on my move from Nashville to Philly in late February 1978. She later told me that the day she visited the station, she immediately sensed an "uneasiness" among station managers. She could tell, she said, by the stares from various producers and managers as they loosely shook her hand.

The way it was explained to me back then was that, after meeting my mother, general manager Larry Pollack was no longer sure that he had satisfied the FCC request for stations to begin hiring more women of color. Pollack reportedly met with news director Alan Nesbitt and assistant news director Bob Feldman, concerned that the young woman they had just hired to anchor the noon news might not be black after all.

I remembered that once in Nashville, during a local

modeling shoot with young women from some of the other TV stations, the man doing makeup—his name was Derrick—asked me if I had ever considered getting work done on my nose.

"Why? Do you think I need a nose job?" I asked.

"It's just that your nose looks a bit ethnic," he replied. "For a white girl, that could be a drawback."

"Well, I'm not white, I'm black," I said.

Derrick turned bright red. "Oh I'm sorry, I had no idea. You, your hair texture is so fine, and your lips . . . I didn't know."

"Hey, it's okay. Not the first time it's happened."

Still, I was in the big city now, I thought; didn't Philadelphia include more nationalities than any of the towns I had lived in before? I had been oblivious to the fact there was any question about my ethnicity in Philly, but my mother had come to sense these things over the years, in lots of towns and cities, as she often found herself the source of racial bewilderment. As it turns out, her intuition was spot on.

It didn't take long for management to find a way to confirm that it had indeed hired a young black woman as its newest news anchor. In the days after mom's station visit, I was called in to Bob Feldman's office, where he asked if I had seen the article about me in the city's largest newspaper, the *Philadelphia Inquirer*. When he handed me the paper, the headline of the article in question read: "WPVI Hires Black Woman to Anchor Its Noon News." He then paused for my reaction. I have to admit I couldn't help intentionally delaying my response—long enough to notice an undeniable moment of awkwardness, a tense instant of uncertainty from Feldman—before I acknowledged how pleased I was with the story.

I remember that episode affectionately today, for in the coming years I would become quite fond of "Uncle Bob" Feldman and general manager Larry Pollack, and appreciative of the genuine caring they demonstrated toward me and other employees at Channel 6.

⁓

Long before there was a question about my "blackness" at WPVI there was the issue of my name. Before Philadelphia, I was Lisa Howard. But I had learned that there was already a Marc Howard at WPVI, with whom I might be working, and that management didn't want any confusion. I was asked if I wouldn't mind choosing another surname with which to be identified on the air in Philadelphia. I thought about it and chose my mother's maiden name, Thomas. So I arrived in Philadelphia as Lisa Thomas.

Six months later, the station hired a new morning talk show host from Buffalo named Dave Thomas. Management quickly explained to Dave that it already had a woman co-anchoring the noon news named Lisa Thomas. Would he choose another on-air name? Dave Thomas became Dave Roberts, although his birth name was Dave Boreanaz. In those days the use of ethnic surnames was discouraged, so Dave was familiar with using a stage name.

While I was delighted with my new job in Philadelphia, it had its challenges, and I suffered some anxiety. My worst fear involved my oldest brother, and it manifested itself in a terrifying dream that had begun shortly after my graduation from Marshall.

Tommy and I play on the train tracks near our school. An old broken-down train that hasn't run in years sits idle on the north end of the tracks. He runs and hides, and I joyfully chase after him. I spot him on the other side of the railroad cars, his head bobbing up and down from window to window. I climb aboard the engine and carefully jump from car to car until I reach the caboose. Then he disappears. Suddenly I become more anxious, the nervousness building the longer my search for him comes up empty.

My worry lingers, turning to absolute fear, then terror, as I realize he is nowhere on or around the train. I slowly walk back to the front of the cars, a horrifying dread consuming me. A glance out of the window—it's dark now. Moonless dark. Only rows of tiny lights illuminate the inside panels of the train. An eerie and ominous stillness hangs over the tracks. For the first time, on the floor of one car, I notice the blood. I can barely move. But I force myself to take one, two more steps. Then I get a glimpse of thick hair. An afro. It's dark blond. No one in all of Dunbar, Institute, or any surrounding town has a head of hair like my brother's. I fall to my knees, not wanting to see, but I do. It is Tommy. No body. Just his decapitated head.

My oldest brother is just 20 months younger than me. We were extremely close during our childhood, and my nightmare about him would haunt me throughout my first job in Oklahoma City, occurring once or twice a week. It happened less frequently when I moved to Nashville, but for one three-week period it occurred almost every night. It always awakened me, and I would be afraid to fall back to sleep.

By the time I moved to Philadelphia, two years later, my ghastly nighttime episodes had waned, but when they did happen, I promised myself I would take a class on the meaning of dreams, certain that if I could only understand why I experienced such a terrifying one, it might go away. I never did, but a psychologist friend later deduced that my frightening dreams were the result of my moving away from home, away from familiar surroundings and people I loved, namely my brother—sort of a separation anxiety. It made sense, and those nightmares began to slowly vanish when I married. They ended entirely following the birth of my first child, Langston.

My friend explained that, more than likely, as I began to establish my own household and assume new familial responsibilities, I became less emotionally attached to my siblings and parents. I accepted that as a reasonable explanation.

TROUBLE AT THE ANCHOR DESK

In other ways, too, my first few months in Philadelphia were stressful. I had never anchored a full half-hour newscast before, not to mention in a market the size of Philadelphia, and while my writing was well above average, I soon discovered that saying the words I wrote out loud was a totally different story. I mispronounced at least a couple of words on air every week, including the names of a host of Philadelphia neighborhoods and surrounding suburbs— places like Conshohocken, Manayunk, Bala Cynwyd and Moyamensing, to name a few.

While viewers seemed to forgive my blunders and were intrigued by my presence (by now my attire had become much more anchor savvy), management was not only restless about my mispronunciations, but excessively concerned about my hair. In those days the "anchor bob" was about the only truly acceptable hairstyle for female TV news anchors. My heavy mane was decidedly too thick and unruly, and much too long, according to my superiors; my goodness, it fell below my shoulders.

I remember vividly the day that assistant news director "Uncle Bob" Feldman called me into his office following one of my noon newscasts. He produced a ruler and meticulously measured both sides of my hair, from my cheekbone to the outer edge of my hairline. Noting that both the right and left sides of my hair were nearly as wide as my face, Feldman strongly suggested that I have it thinned.

The station sent me to a renowned hair stylist on the other side of City Avenue, in one of those towns I had mispronounced during a newscast. I had had my hair straightened before but never liked the outcome. Now, after having it thinned, there was only one way I could wear it: in an anchor "bob." It was at least two years before my hair was what I considered normal again.

JIMBO

Thank God for co-anchors! On the brief, three-minute morning "cut-ins" that I anchored in Nashville and Oklahoma, I worked solo, and I was usually the writer and producer of my own reports. Having someone share the anchor desk, especially for a half-hour newscast, was a dream. And for a fledgling anchorwoman, having that someone be Jim O'Brien was the best thing that could have happened.

He was born James Oldham in Galveston, Texas. In 1970, eight years before I arrived in the City of Brotherly Love, Jim moved to Philadelphia and took the city by storm. After six years as a radio disc jockey at WFIL, O'Brien joined WPVI as a sports anchor. He soon became the weatherman and a beloved local celebrity.

Rival stations would eventually flaunt their more modern technology for weather reports, but Channel 6 knew it only needed "Jimbo," his loony sense of humor and his unique way of expressing himself. Along with his low-tech weather map and pointer, Jim had sunshine stickers that he called the "good guys" and stick-on gray clouds known as the "bad guys."

"Fuck 'em," he would say to me, acknowledging my frustration those first six months with the Action News team. Besides totally changing my look with the thinning of my hair, management kept reminding me about my pronunciations and suggesting that something be done to help me lose my West Virginia twang. They would eventually locate a speech therapist for me. Dr. Julia Wing from Temple University taught me how to breathe from my diaphragm when speaking and how to deliver the news with a more universal dialect.

"They're messin' with your head," Jim insisted, suggesting that I block out my worries and simply focus on the newscast. He told me that except for the occasional bungling of street and town names, I was a flawless news reader who had the extraordinary talent of delivering the news in a relaxed, informal manner. He encouraged me not to let the criticisms get in the way of that.

At one point, I brought to work a list of local streets, boroughs, cities, most frequent Philly phrases, you name it—anything that I thought might trip me up during a newscast—and asked Jim to practice with me. He quickly agreed, and we became professionally engaged in my pursuit of proficiency. Jim helped me until my on-air flubs became nonexistent. Almost. And then he taught me how to handle the flubs, to make them appear just as they would in an ordinary conversation. I haven't received more sapient advice since.

After those first few difficult months, I began to thrive at Channel 6. I loved the reporting, being out, visiting Philly's neighborhoods and meeting a multifarious mixture of people. And I was becoming more confident at the anchor desk, partly because working with Jim was a welcome challenge, and also a blast. I never knew what unscripted and hilarious moment he would bring to our newscast. As soon as he knew I was secure in my co-anchor role, he loved to have fun on the set at my expense.

During one noontime newscast, unbeknown to me, Jim modified a word in my teleprompter copy. Imagine my astonishment when, as I reported about the Schlitz Beer Company, what came out of my mouth on live television was "Shits Beer." Jim didn't even try to stifle his laughter; while the camera remained focused on me, he was off his seat and on the floor in hysterics. He later told me he was proud of the way I recovered.

And then there were days when I could give it right back. One winter afternoon after an unexpected seven-inch snowfall, Jim wrapped up a story on the forecast and tossed to me with the question, "Well, Leese, were you surprised this morning?"

The look on his face at my reply was priceless.

"Not really, Jim," I said. "I thought I'd wake up to at least eight inches."

MEETING DR. LAURY

I had canceled two scheduled dinners with Bill Laury because of work assignments and was nearly an hour late for my actual first date with him for the same reason.

My friend and colleague Vernon Odom had introduced me to my husband-to-be. The two lived in the same apartment complex near our station, and Vern had set us up on a blind date.

It was the first time I had been to the celebrated Moshulu, the world's largest and oldest square-rigged sailing vessel that's still afloat. Permanently docked at Philadelphia's Penn's Landing along the Delaware River waterfront, the refurbished ship is the world's only legendary Tall Ship that has a restaurant.

Bill was sitting at one of the first tables as I entered the dining room, and I was relieved to see his expression change from one of annoyance to full approval as I approached.

We had a night to remember, but what I recall most about that first date was how delighted I was that Bill initially had no idea that I was a local newscaster; he had never seen me on TV. I had had my fill of meeting guys who were enamored by so-called local celebrities, men who were solely interested in having a sampling of TV eye candy to accompany them to the neighborhood club.

Dr. William Laury was different; he hadn't known who I was because he didn't have time to watch local TV news. He had recently started his medical practice in Mt. Airy, a diverse neighborhood in northwest Philadelphia, just a short bus ride from Center City.

Bill was smart and funny, and an easy conversationalist. Plus, I thought he was good-looking in a glamorous, sporty kind of way. He looked like a cross between Hollywood actor Billy Dee Williams and former major league baseball right fielder Reggie Jackson.

Born in Richmond, Virginia, Bill had grown up poor in Chester, Delaware County, and attended Cheyney State College. He'd lost his mother to cancer his freshman year, and then worked two and three jobs to put himself through medical school at Jefferson University Hospital. He'd been accepted to the prestigious McGill University Medical School in Montreal, Canada, for an elective in obstetrics and gynecology. He later chose internal medicine as his specialty.

The second thing I remember about Bill on that first night was that he must have really liked me because, instead of asking me for a second date, he attempted to line me up for the next three weeks. We laugh about that still.

Bill and I dated for a little more than a year, then married in the summer of 1980 back in my home state of West Virginia. A host of his family members and my colleagues and friends from Action News drove the eight-plus hours through mountainous terrain to be there. The station sent a crew to film the event, and my wedding aired as a half-hour special on the public affairs show *Visions*. WPVI's main anchor, Jim Gardner, hosted the program.

Following my marriage, I decided to add Bill's surname to mine on air. It was common in those days for news-women and businesswomen to combine their last names with their husbands', and thus I became known as Lisa Thomas-Laury to our viewers.

LISA IN LONDON

From my wedding to the Royal Wedding: The year following my marriage to Bill, I was chosen to cover one of the biggest stories of my career. The joining of Charles, Prince of Wales, and Lady Diana Spencer in matrimony on July 29, 1981, in London, England, was dubbed the wedding of the century. It drew an estimated global TV audience of 750 million people.

I was there for one week, with executive producer Cheryl Fair and cameraman Bob Pruitt. We had a grueling schedule, mostly because of the five-hour time difference. Local television didn't yet have the capability to air live video reports from around the world. However, I did live phone-in reports, in addition to filing preproduced news "packages" via satellite.

I reported on everything from Diana's decision to omit the word "obey" from her traditional wedding vows to Philadelphia's "The Three Degrees," Prince Charles's favorite singing group. He had chosen them to perform at a pre-wedding party.

When I met the group at a London Hotel for a sit-down interview, I realized that only two Degrees were in town to perform for the prince. Helen Scott and Valerie Holiday were delightful, chatting with me about their careers and their relationship with the prince, having also been asked to perform at his 30th birthday party three years earlier. Sheila Ferguson, the third Degree, was home in Philadelphia, pregnant with twins.

No doubt the station had thought that I, still the newlywed whose own wedding our viewers had watched in record numbers on Channel 6, would be the ideal reporter for this assignment. Before I left London, I was certain I had come upon a sign that demonstrated just that. As my crew and I approached a pub in West London where we had arranged to do a feature story, we noticed the sign above the Thomas Truck Rental Company. Trucks are known as lorries in England, and the sign read, "Lease a Thomas Lorry." I was convinced that I was right where I was supposed to be, doing what I was destined to do.

PHILLY IS HOME

When I first arrived in Philadelphia, I thought I would move on in a few years to New York City, the country's number-one television market. I had started at Channel

3 in Huntington, moved on to Channel 4 in Oklahoma City, then TV-5 in Nashville, and was now at Channel 6. It seemed only appropriate that I would end my career at ABC, TV-7, in New York.

But even before I met Bill, I became smitten with Philadelphia. And Jim O'Brien would always say to me, "What on earth do you want to go to New York for? You're a star here; you'll be nothing more than a little fish in a big pond in New York."

As much as I wanted to anchor a prime-time newscast, I knew the noon news was as good as it would probably get at WPVI because practically no one who worked there ever left. Jim Gardner was solid at six and eleven, Marc and Jim could be a team forever at five. I had a chance to fill in as an anchor at five when Jim or Marc was on vacation or called in sick, and I decided I could live with that. O'Brien was right; I pretty much had the best of both worlds in Philly—family and a great career.

GOODBYE, JIMBO

It was Sunday afternoon, September 25, 1983, a few minutes before one o'clock, when I got the call from "Uncle Bob" Feldman. Bill and I were shopping with our year-old son, Langston, at the Deptford Mall near Blackwood, New Jersey, across the bridge from Philly.

Jim had been killed in a skydiving accident in New Hanover Township.

Bill and I immediately headed for our car. My mind drifted to two days earlier, in the studio, when Jim talked to me and Marc about his plans to skydive over the weekend, challenging both of us to join him one day. We joked about how that probably wouldn't happen, but we reminded him to be safe and wished him Godspeed.

That was a generation ago now, but nearly everyone in the Delaware Valley remembers where they were on that fateful day and what they were doing. Our viewers were devastated; they felt as though they had lost a close family friend.

At Channel 6 we *had* lost a cherished member of our TV family.

Not a year has passed since that I don't think of Jim on September 25, especially how he took me under his wing when I was most vulnerable.

Several weeks after Jim's death, I realized that the passing of this enigmatic yet bighearted man, who offered me so much in the way of support and inspiration, would be a watershed moment in my career. I assumed Jim's role as five o'clock anchor with Marc Howard and took over his duties hosting the Fourth of July and Thanksgiving Day parades with Dave Roberts.

LIFE IS GOOD—MOSTLY

When I say that the next 20 years at Channel 6, and in my life, were almost idyllic, I mean that Philly was exceptionally good to me.

Viewers in the region embraced me, and Bill became one of the top doctors in the black community. We had the usual ups and downs of married life, with me juggling my career and family, and Bill dealing with the pressures of running his own medical practice. But we loved Philadelphia, its surrounding neighborhoods and the people in the Delaware Valley. We felt blessed with the life we were living, and we were grateful for the love we shared and for our two healthy and active sons. Life was splendid. Except for one terrifying incident in the station parking lot in 1990.

Sports anchor Scott Palmer and I were leaving Channel 6, following our 5:30 p.m. broadcast on January 4, when I spotted a man walking quickly toward us. As he got closer, I noticed he was young, probably in his early twenties, with massive arms and an expressionless face. I thought he was going to continue right past us, but before I could ask, "Scott, do you know who this guy is?" he suddenly pivoted and punched me in the face. Hard. Full force.

The next thing I remember is Scott trying to help me up. As I rose to my feet, I heard the speeding car on the other side of the parking lot, its tires screeching. It turned and sped our way. Scott yanked me between two parked cars as the attacker blasted past us.

Simultaneously, sports director Don Tollefson, also leaving work, noticed the commotion, and after a brief recap from Scott, jumped in his Corvette and attempted to follow the suspect. By now I could feel the blood dripping from a small cut on my cheekbone below my left eye. Scott walked me back into the station, where someone had already called 911.

After I was rushed to the hospital, I learned that Don had caught up with my attacker on the highway, close enough to get the license plate number and contact police on his CB radio. Officers arrested the suspect at his home within the hour.

My cut required only four stitches, but I also suffered a grossly swollen eye and severe bruises around my eye and nose. And my cornea was scratched where my contact had been knocked out. I was off the air for two weeks.

I learned later that my attacker suffered from paranoid schizophrenia and had stopped taking his medicine for the disorder. He told police that when he watched me on TV, he would continually hear my voice reprimanding him, even after he turned his television off. He said he came to the station to shut me up.

After this incident, there were questions about the responsibility of television stations to protect their employees, especially those on air who are promoted as viewer-friendly and approachable. Does a TV station have an obligation to protect its news personalities from viewers who might be violent?

There had been other incidents involving the harassment of newscasters in the tristate area, but none had been physically attacked. Nationally, a woman newscaster had been murdered by a deranged viewer who stalked her at her TV station, followed her home and then abducted and killed her. In my case, the perpetrator had waited for me for three hours in the Channel 6 parking lot.

Eventually, my station erected a fence around its property, installed an electronic gate and hired 24/7 guards to monitor the entrance. Since then, there have been no major security issues.

In court, my attacker, whose hobby was body building, pleaded no defense to simple assault and recklessly endangering the life of another person. A judge found him guilty by reason of mental illness and sentenced him to four years' psychiatric probation. He was ordered to stay away from me and resume taking his medication.

⁓

Despite that one ugly encounter, I was deeply happy with my life. By late summer 2001, I had been reporting and anchoring the news in Philadelphia for 23 years. I was making more money at age 47 than I could have ever imagined. Most important, I loved what I was doing.

Physically, I was in the best shape of my life. My routine, established in the mid-1990s, included a daily workout after driving my boys to school. Three days a week, my exercise trainer, Bobbi, would meet me at my home after my school drop-off for a more rigorous exercise regimen and a power walk around my neighborhood.

My older son, Langston, was about to enter college at Brown University in Providence, Rhode Island, the first in our family to be accepted to an Ivy League school. My younger, Leland, was heading into Upper School at Episcopal Academy in Merion, Pennsylvania, where he played football and tennis. I wasn't yet an empty nester, but I was excited about the prospect of finally having an opportunity to devote a little more time to me.

I had no idea that my ideal world was about to shatter.

CHAPTER THREE

LIFE THROWS ME
A CURVE

It was in the early spring of 2001 that Bobbi and I first noticed an inexplicable weakness in my feet and ankles. It was taking longer and more effort for me to make it up the inclines on my power walks, and I had begun to feel a slight numbness and tingling in my feet.

Initially, when I detected the strange sensations and soreness, I did what most busy professional women with children do when something's not quite right physically: I ignored it. I thought the aches and throbbing might be due to calluses on the balls of my feet, instigated by my power walking. Eventually I visited my nail salon for a spa pedicure, asking that extra attention be paid to removing the calluses and massaging my feet. Still, the numbness and pain persisted, then worsened. The tingling later became more consistent, with a feeling of sharp "pins and needles."

By this time my feet had turned grayish in color, and my ankles were dark red with patches of blue and gray, as though they were bruised and inflamed. Bill arranged for me to see a podiatrist he knew. The doctor suggested I might have ganglions—small cystic tumors—or a mass of nerve tissue in both feet. He recommended that I get steroid injections between my toes. But the treatments did nothing to relieve my symptoms, and my ankles were getting progressively weaker.

My mother, extended family, coworkers and friends tried to encourage me, suggesting that my baffling symptoms would eventually disappear. "Keep the faith," they would tell me. "You'll get some answers soon, and you'll be back to normal in no time."

"Keep the faith." I thought about that phrase and remembered James Baldwin's book *The Evidence of Things Not Seen*. He took that title from the Epistle to the Hebrews: "Faith is the substance of things hoped for, the evidence of things not seen."

I remained hopeful.

MORE QUESTIONS THAN ANSWERS

Bill arranged for me to visit a local neurologist, Dr. Jahangir Maleki, at the Medical College of Pennsylvania. Dr. Maleki performed an electromyogram exam (EMG), a painful nerve conduction study.

In the examining room in my hospital gown, I was asked to lie on a table and relax the muscles in my legs and arms. Flat metal disc electrodes were attached to my limbs, my chest and neck. An electrode with a two-inch needle connected to a recording machine was then inserted into a muscle. Several quick electric shocks or pulses in varying degrees of intensity were administered to my nerve, and the time it took for the muscle to contract in response to the electrical pulse was recorded. The needle, which, to a person with her glasses off, closely resembled a knitting needle, was moved a number of times to record activity in different areas of various muscles.

I've had numerous other EMG exams over the years, and I literally jump at the thought of the procedure. A series of such 90-minute tests is not pleasant, but we hoped that first one would provide some answers.

And it did. The initial EMG showed that I had lost about 30% of the strength in my lower extremities. Dr. Maleki called it "bilateral polyneuropathy" that was progressing in my feet and legs. He was the first doctor to discover that I had a serious medical problem. However, the EMG and additional tests failed to show why. There could be a number of different reasons for the growing weakness in my feet and legs. The situation was baffling and utterly discouraging.

THE DOCTORS' BEST EFFORTS

My next visit was with Dr. Edward Kenton, former chief of neurology at Lankenau Hospital in Wynnewood, where both my sons had been born. Dr. Kenton had been a mentor to my husband in medical school. He is a small-framed, dark-skinned and fiercely intelligent black man who rose to his prestigious position because of his wealth of knowledge and his extremely high level of self-confidence.

Although he had seen only five cases in his career, Dr. Kenton believed I was suffering from a rare plasma cell disorder known as POEMS syndrome, Crow-Fukase syndrome or Takatsuki disease. Doctor Kenton explained to me and my husband that I had three of the five most prominent symptoms experienced by people with the condition.

POEMS is an acronym, each letter representing one of the five main features of the illness:

P for polyneuropathy, a degenerative state of the nervous system or nerves; my polyneuropathy was bilateral, in both feet and ankles.

O for organomegaly, or enlarged organs; I did not have any oversized organs at the time.

E for endocrinopathy, a disease of the endocrine glands; I had not yet developed an endocrine disorder.

M for monoclonal gammopathy, signified by an abnormal protein in the blood; my anomalous protein had elevated my platelet count from a normal of approximately 150,000–400,000 to upwards of 1.4 million. The excess protein is caused by an overabundance of a particular set or "clone" of plasma cells in the bone marrow.

S for skin abnormalities; hyperpigmentation had become a problem for me, my skin turning almost grayish blue, and I had developed tiny angiomas, or tumors composed of blood vessels, on areas of my skin.

I had three of the five major symptoms. Dr. Kenton noted that POEMS syndrome was a precancerous condition and that it was important to get the proper treatment as soon as possible. However, he couldn't follow my case because he was about to leave the area to become director of the Stroke Prevention/Intervention Research Program at Morehouse School of Medicine in Atlanta. Since a plasma cell disorder is at the root of POEMS, he referred me to a hematologist at Lankenau, a man who initially agreed with Dr. Kenton that my symptoms were consistent with POEMS syndrome. He started me on a course of steroids and a chemotherapy pill.

I began my new medical regimen as my sons were approaching spring break at Episcopal Academy. We had planned a family trip to Las Vegas, which was making a concerted effort to become more family-friendly. Despite my sudden health problems, I didn't want to disappoint my kids. Plus, Bill was due for a much-needed break from work, and I welcomed a respite from back-to-back doctors' visits.

So we checked into Mandalay Bay, which boasted of having the most popular kid attractions on the Las Vegas strip, including the Shark Reef Aquarium, which had debuted the previous year. We all loved it. The hotel also had an incredible water entertainment park with a wave pool and a man-made sandy beach.

Bill and I rented a cabana, stocked with portable fans and a TV, and we relaxed with the boys for hours a day. I made sure to keep my feet raised as often as possible to keep them from swelling excessively. However, one late morning, after Leland and I slept in and were on our way to join his dad and Lang on the "beach," Lee noticed that my big toe was bleeding. I had stubbed my toe on the threshold leaving our hotel suite but hadn't thought much of it. Now Lee ran ahead to the pool to bring back a towel to wrap my toe. I assured him it didn't hurt, but when we cleaned off the blood, we noticed my toenail had been ripped off. Just the thought of this happening made me a little nauseous. A member of the hotel staff got us some cleansing wipes, gauze and tape, and Lee helped me wrap the toe tightly to stop the bleeding.

When we reached our cabana, Bill was disturbed by what had happened and, noticing my toe was slightly swollen, insisted I soak it in ice water. We were concerned that I hadn't felt anything but a slight pulling and some pressure when I lost my nail. Still, I assured Bill I was fine and encouraged him to postpone worrying about it until we returned home.

After this discussion, I thought I might be feeling *some* pain; it felt like my toe was pulsing, but I wasn't sure. It certainly wasn't anything severe, so I popped a couple of Advils and soaked up some more sun.

Come nighttime, it was show time. "Mystère" by Cirque du Soleil at Bellagio was out of this world, but the boys' favorite was Siegfried and Roy at the Mirage. As magicians, Siegfried and Roy wove their magic with the magic of nature. They were master illusionists who made various things, including magnificent feline kings and queens of the jungle, disappear, then reappear. We had great seats, relatively close to the stage, and the beauty of those white lions and tigers was mesmerizing, almost hypnotic.

Two years later, their captivating act came to an abrupt end when one of their beloved cats, a seven-year-old male white tiger named Montecore, bit into Roy Horn's neck and dragged him off stage during a live show. Roy was critically injured but survived, and he insisted that no harm come to Montecore. Investigators never determined what caused the tiger to attack.

⌒

Before our Vegas spring vacation, Dr. Kenton had referred me to a neurologist at Johns Hopkins Medical Center in Baltimore. My first visit to him was in the summer of 2002.

From the outset, I didn't care for this doctor. An enormous, odd-looking man, considered to be among the elite in his field, he spoke primarily to my husband, as though I didn't have the intelligence to understand what he was saying.

After an examination and a half day of testing, he and my hematologist at Lankenau Hospital both dismissed Dr. Kenton's diagnosis of POEMS. They agreed that my symptoms were more aligned with CIDP, chronic inflammatory demyelinating polyneuropathy, an acquired immune-mediated inflammatory disorder of the peripheral nervous system. An autoimmune disease, CIDP is closely related to Guillain-Barré syndrome and is considered the chronic counterpart to that acute disease.

The two doctors concurred that, for the next six months, I should follow a regimen of Imuran (an immunosuppressant medication), steroids and plasmapheresis (a blood-cleansing treatment). On my next visit to Johns Hopkins, the neurologist declared he was pleased with my "improvement." However, I was certain my condition was worsening.

Although I was doing everything in my power to continue with my news anchor duties, by September of 2002, a little more than a year after my first symptoms appeared, my balance had become a significant problem. It was more difficult for me to walk and stand without holding on to something or someone. While I was moving around the newsroom working on my story that would air that night, it wasn't uncommon to see me grabbing the wall or a shoulder along the way. Still, there were some days when the steroids masked my symptoms and I felt briefly that my condition might be improving.

Then there were days when I felt completely fatigued. It would take all my strength to get through a shortened workday and return home to rest. Bill was assuming more of our daily meal preparations and other household chores.

ON LEAVE

In November 2002 my condition began to noticeably deteriorate. While no one at work said anything to me, I observed, while viewing my air checks or recordings of my newscasts, that my anchoring lacked energy and enthusiasm. I had also developed "foot drop" and had fallen several times at work and at home. While I made the effort to raise my feet slightly as I walked, I was constantly stumbling, especially on uneven sidewalks and irregular terrain.

My decision to take a short-term medical leave from my job that November was not a difficult one. I knew I needed to concentrate on getting an accurate diagnosis, and I didn't expect to be out for long, certainly not the entire six months I was allotted. An article in the *Philadelphia Inquirer* said I would be "off the air" for the next several months for a nerve disorder that was curable. I'm still not sure who told the newspaper that my disease was curable. Station management was supportive, assuring me that my anchor position would be waiting for me when I returned.

It was my first week on medical leave, and when the packages arrived, the tears flowed. Oprah sent a beautiful silver box filled with Kiehl's skin care products and a handwritten note. That same day, lovely flowers arrived from Renee Chenault-Fattah of NBC News, and the next day, flowers from Ukee Washington of Philadelphia's CBS affiliate. I was extremely touched that Queen O, and even my competitors in the industry, had thought of me, along with my close friends and ABC colleagues and viewers.

I spent much of my time during those first few months away from work, seeing doctors and on my computer, trying to better understand what the doctors couldn't explain. What *was* causing the muscle weakness and nerve pain in my legs, as well as the tingling and severe burning sensation in my feet? Was it CIDP, as my doctors suggested, and my husband and I now doubted? Was it POEMS syndrome? Or something else? Bill and I thought my current doctors had not looked closely enough at the possibility that POEMS syndrome might be the culprit.

I spent a lot of time looking up everything I could about the disorder, its symptoms, treatments, their side effects, etc. And its victims' prognoses: at that point, people diagnosed with POEMS had a life expectancy of 7 to 11 years from the time the first symptoms appeared. That was with treatment; without treatment, the survival expectancy was only 3 to 5 years.

Suddenly it hit me. *My life expectancy?* They are talking about how long it will be before I *die* from this thing? All the more reason my doctors needed to get it right! If I had CIDP, I needed the correct medication to treat it. If I had POEMS, I could not waste time. I needed an accurate diagnosis. You have two choices when you arrive in that arena where your illness is laid out naked and raw before you, its ugly truth exposed. You can either succumb to the unnerving reality that it could lead to your death, or you can fight to continue to live.

By now, unlike my lack of sensation in Vegas, the tops of my toes and feet had actually become so hypersensitive that it was painful to have the sheets touch them in bed at night. I slept on my back with my legs raised and the sheets tucked under my ankles. My feet and toes were always super-cold, so I wore Bill's thermal socks.

In contrast, I had very little feeling on the soles of my feet. During the sizzling summer of 2002, I had walked barefoot in my driveway with my miniature schnauzer Pepper, unable to feel the intense heat from the asphalt. That episode badly burned the plantar surface of my feet and bottoms of my toes.

DOCTORS' EGOS GET IN THE WAY

On July 8, 2003, approximately six months since my last visit, we were once again on our way to Johns Hopkins. As we turned off Interstate 95 in Baltimore, I felt my stomach begin to tighten. I knew we would wind through blocks of trash-strewn streets and graffiti-marked buildings before reaching the hospital's parking garage on Orleans Street. If we were lucky, we'd find a handicapped space on a floor below the top exposed level, and there would be a wheel-chair at the garage elevator. It was our lucky day. We found a handicapped spot and several wheelchairs in the elevator vestibule.

The lobby of Johns Hopkins is modern and spacious; the receptionists and staff, extremely professional and cour-teous. There are many wonderful doctors who work there. My husband had previously received treatment there, and several friends had experienced exceptional care from phy-sicians and nurses at Hopkins. I was less fortunate.

We had been sitting in the waiting area for only about 10 minutes when he arrived, walking flat-footed and flop-pily down the hall. I had nicknamed him "Dr. Prick." In hindsight it seems incredibly juvenile, and please under-stand that I don't normally use such unflattering words to describe anyone. But in his case, and in my frame of mind, I felt it was well deserved.

He greeted me with the same forced smile as always, only this time he was even more condescending. As I walked ahead of him and Bill toward his office, he observed—erro-neously, I thought—how much I had improved from my last visit: "She definitely looks stronger, and her gait has improved significantly." With such a decisive conclusion at first glance, before any actual examination, I wondered: should I really believe he remembered how I walked six months ago?

Once in his office, we were left with a medical fellow who conducted a brief physical examination and updated my condition on paper. When "Dr. Prick" returned, I was subjected to another cursory exam, followed by equally inane comments.

"Good strength, she's stronger above the knees."

"I never had any weakness above the knees," I countered.

"Spread your fingers . . . close them . . . push against my fist. Good! The prednisone is certainly having a positive impact on her."

"Bullshit," I said under my breath.

He continued his premature declarations of my unsubstantiated improvement. "Yes, her hands are also both stronger."

"They never were a real problem," I responded.

"I definitely think the current course of prednisone and plasmapheresis is having a positive effect," he said, totally ignoring me.

"You are not listening!" I said, raising my voice. "I am not getting better. I told you I feel weaker!" I was almost screaming now, and on the verge of tears.

Bill tried to quiet me. "Lisa, don't get upset, honey."

"How can I not get upset? Every time I come here, he says I'm improving, despite my telling him otherwise. He presses my hands, knees and feet and tells me they're stronger when there's no way he could know that by just touching me. Plus *I know* they are weaker!"

"Dr. Prick" then turned to my husband and, in an annoyingly calm voice, suggested, "This is understandable; I think I'll order her some Zoloft."

"I'm not depressed, I'm pissed!" I shouted. My reaction was both visceral and one of complete exasperation. "Zoloft won't fix that; only a doctor who acknowledges me and listens to me will. And another thing, my *feet and legs* are impaired, not my ears. I can hear, and I'm not stupid. You don't have to direct all your comments to my husband; you can talk to me!"

He turned to Bill once more. "I will give you some time, privately."

"Punk ass, shit-faced coward"—this time I came close to cursing out loud.

Before I left Hopkins that day, "Dr. Prick" suggested that I see a neurologist at the University of Pennsylvania in conjunction with visits to him, so that I wouldn't have to make as many trips to Baltimore. That was welcome news to me.

CHAPTER FOUR

A MYSTERIOUS
ILLNESS

I WILL ALWAYS remember the date, August 16, 2003. The big international story that day was the death of former Ugandan dictator Idi Amin. I watched on my television screen as jubilant Ugandans celebrated, leaping and dancing in the streets. I rejoiced with them but kept focusing on their legs and feet.

How remarkable it was, I thought, that these Third World men, women and children—dirt-poor, their clothes filthy and shredded, their bellies distended from hunger—could move so happily and effortlessly. *They could wiggle their toes!* And I was facing the increasing inability to move my own.

A SECOND AND THIRD OPINION

That was the day, August 16, 2003, that I had an appointment with Dr. Terry Heiman-Patterson, a neurologist at Hahnemann University Hospital, who was able to offer some hope about my illness. She was easy to talk with, and she discussed my condition with compassion and understanding. While she agreed that CIDP was a possibility, she began exploring the diagnosis suggested to me so many months before—POEMS syndrome.

She also wanted me to meet another of her patients, Todd MacCulloch, who had until recently played center for the Philadelphia 76ers. Todd was suffering from a baffling illness that had forced him off the basketball court. The doctors who were treating our disorders thought both Todd and I were suffering from CIDP.

At seven feet tall, Todd was truly a gentle giant. He had joined the Sixers in 2000, then left following the NBA finals, only to return in the 2002 trade that saw Dikembe Mutombo go to the New Jersey Nets. Todd was then sidelined halfway through the 2002–2003 season with foot and coordination problems.

Todd told Bill and me that he had a constant stinging pain in his feet, exactly what I was experiencing. He said it would range from a pins-and-needles sensation to pain so severe that he could barely walk or even concentrate. We agreed that we both might be suffering from the same ailment, but neither of us was sure that we had CIDP. Todd had sought out Heiman-Patterson, as I had, for a second opinion.

A few weeks after meeting Todd, Bill and I got a third opinion, from the doctor at Penn to whom my Johns Hopkins specialist had referred me. After a thorough examination and study of my records from Hopkins and Lankenau Hospital, the Penn neurologist concurred that I was suffering from CIDP. He suggested that I continue with my plasmapheresis treatments, and he reinstated my prednisone, which had been stopped due to unfavorable side effects, at a lower dose. The doctor at Penn also said he had some misgivings about the effectiveness of the immunosuppressant Imuran I was taking, but he decided not to discontinue the drug.

Simultaneously I was being encouraged by my gastroenterologist, Dr. Gary Newman, and a second hematologist/oncologist, Dr. Steve Cohen, both with Main Line Health, to pay a visit to the Mayo Clinic in Rochester, Minnesota. Dr. Newman had discovered a wonderful physician there, Dr. Angela Dispenzieri, also a hematologist, who he said had more experience with patients like me. Instead of an autoimmune disease, the umbrella label for a host of neu-rological/muscular conditions, Dr. Newman believed I was suffering from a plasma cell dyscrasia disorder. Also, Dr. Dispenzieri had written the standard of care for POEMS syndrome, which Dr. Newman, Dr. Cohen and Bill and I all thought should not be dismissed as a possible cause for my symptoms.

BACK TO WORK
BUT NOT FOR LONG

My husband and I put the Mayo Clinic on our list of prior-ities, but in the months after I was referred there, I actually returned to work for a short time.

By then I had seen a physiatrist, not to be confused with a psychiatrist. A physiatrist specializes in physical medi-cine and rehabilitation, and this one strongly suggested I begin wearing leg braces to support my ankles and allevi-ate the foot drop that had led to some pretty bad falls. I had initially resisted, until one day as I brought takeout home from a nearby Olive Garden, my foot clipped the limen in the passageway leading to my mudroom from the garage, and I fell flat on my face, splattering our dinner all over the floor.

The braces were like open-air boots that fit just below my knee. They included a foot piece, molded to conform to my feet, that slipped into the length of my shoe. The brace strapped around my upper calves and ankles. I no-ticed immediately the improvement in my foot drop and my balance.

Still, returning to work had been the last thing I felt able to do. I was weak and tired most of the time. But my general manager had asked if I thought I had the strength to come in just a few hours a day and anchor the five o'clock news. He offered to send a car to take me to and from the station. I thought I'd be a wimp to say no, so I shopped for a good wig (as my hair had now thinned considerably) and returned to the anchor desk in September 2003.

At work I found inspiration from a longtime colleague, our sports director, Gary Papa, who had recently been diagnosed with stage 4 prostate cancer. He was unusually upbeat and talkative about his condition, and this seemed to give him the strength he needed to cope. His optimism was infectious, and on days when I was feeling particularly somber, just seeing him walk my way would lift my spirits. Gary would tell me, "I'm praying for you, Leese—that they'll nail this thing down for you, so you can attack it head on, the way I'm fighting the big C."

In my mind, if Gary could do it, so could I. However, there were many days when I felt more out of place on the job than I'd thought would ever be possible. Not even in 1978, during those first months at WPVI when I was butchering the names of streets and towns, did I feel this uneasy. I was enormously uncomfortable being back at work. Just six months earlier, I had looked much healthier than I was, but now the difference in my appearance had become conspicuous. Though I had lost a significant amount of weight, the steroids had made my face fuller, and it appeared even plumper on TV. Also, I hated my wig. Not only did I think it looked artificial on the air, it was hot, and it made me perspire under the warm studio lights.

I tried to give it my best, but viewers called and wrote in, asking if I was all right. I recognized that most of their queries were sincere, but they made me terribly self-conscious.

One evening following a newscast, in November 2003, only two and a half months after my return to the anchor desk, my news director, Carla Carpenter, called me in to her office to say my voice sounded frail on the air. I hadn't noticed, and neither had my co-anchor. But she suggested I take a few days off to see if I might be coming down with a cold.

I knew in my heart it was more than that. Yet as I left the station that night, I had no idea it would be my last day at Action News for more than two years.

CHAPTER FIVE

BE YOUR OWN
ADVOCATE

ONE THING I have learned during my health crisis, and want to encourage everyone reading this to remember—Never hesitate to get a second, third or fourth opinion! If you don't agree with or understand something your doctor has told you, ask him or her to explain it better. Ask *again* if the answer is still not clear to you. In retrospect, I wish I had been even more vocal about what I was feeling in my gut.

Both Bill and I regret that we didn't seek other opinions sooner. I cannot emphasize enough—YOU MUST BE AN ADVOCATE for your own health care. DEMAND TO KNOW! My husband and I thought at the time that we had asked all the right questions, but we wish we had asked more.

Bill recalls an incident in his childhood when his mother was a fierce advocate for his health and well-being. About nine years old, he was spending the summer on his family's farm in Buckingham, Virginia, when he was bitten by a water moccasin on his right hand. His mother and uncles rushed him to the local doctor, who lanced the snake bite. But seeing how swollen and discolored the hand had become, the doctor announced to Bill's mother, "Bernice, I think your boy's gonna lose that hand."

Bill's mom was defiant. "Oh no, he's not," she declared confidently, walking out of the doctor's office.

That night, Bill's mother and her sisters sat up all night, keeping his hand submerged in ice. His mother's brother used a pocket knife to again slice the skin around the snake bite and squeeze out more of the venom.

Silly faces for the camera: my brother Tommy with me, Easter Sunday, 1959.

On our best behavior: with mom on Easter Sunday, 1959.

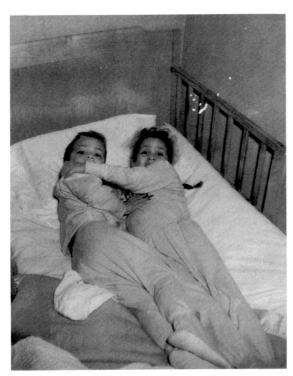

Tommy and I in our bunny pajamas, Easter night, 1959.

My first-grade school photo, age 6.

My fourth-grade school photo. I was in fourth grade when I started writing and producing school plays.

At age 24, I appeared in *Ebony* magazine as the youngest TV news anchor in Philadelphia.

I became popular on the speaking circuit. Here I am at Saint Joseph's University in 1980.

With Jim O'Brien in 1979, one year after I joined the Action News team.

Interviewing Senator Ted Kennedy in downtown Philadelphia, 1979.

My grandfather, "Papa," had been an important role model for me and my brothers.

A happy but tearful bride: July 12, 1980.

As her name implies, Blossom Howard was a beautiful and loving mother and grandmother. Here she is with baby Langston and me in 1982.

In my early Channel 6 years with Marc Howard and Jim O'Brien. (Photo credit: WPVI-TV)

Bill and I on vacation in the Bahamas.

At a White House luncheon with President Reagan in 1986.

I learned so much from co-anchor Marc Howard. Here we are in 1986.

Bill and I relaxing at home, 1994.

By morning, his hand had begun returning to its normal color, and the swelling had subsided considerably. Bill made a full recovery, and he often repeats his story to his patients as a reminder to them to be diligent and all-inquiring about their health.

AN ILLNESS IN DISGUISE

On my fourth visit to the Penn neurologist, he suggested that he might try a different treatment on me: IVIG, intravenous immunoglobulin. IVIG contains naturally occurring antibodies that are obtained from healthy volunteers. They would be administered through one of my veins, and the process would take several hours.

The doctor told me that IVIG was the only drug with FDA, Canadian and European approval for the treatment of CIDP. The idea was to boost my immune deficiency by giving me antibodies that my system could not make on its own. But, in the end, the doctor decided against IVIG because he thought the risks, having to do with my own abnormal immunoglobulin, might outweigh the benefits.

Also on this fourth visit, and because my illness had forced me to leave work a second time, I asked the Penn doctor when he thought I might be well enough to return to work again. His reply astounded me. He said he thought I should remain on disability indefinitely. I immediately asked why; did he think my condition was hopeless? He said that he thought it would be extremely difficult for me to keep up with things at work. Really?

I was determined to prove him wrong.

For the next six months, I was told, I would be treated with the steroid prednisone, plasmapheresis (the blood-cleansing treatment) and Imuran. On this regimen I initially felt I might be improving. My trio of specialists had nearly convinced me that I was.

But soon I developed additional symptoms—extreme and more consistent fatigue and an enlarged liver, which was a fourth sign of POEMS (organomegaly). As a doctor, my husband explained to me that often the symptoms of some illnesses mimic those of other diseases, and it can be difficult to distinguish between one disorder and another.

Yet, in my case, we knew that Dr. Kenton, the former chief of neurology at the same hospital as my hematologist, had already suspected that I was suffering from POEMS syndrome. He had noted, for one thing, that my platelet count was off the chart. A normal platelet count ranges somewhere between 150,000 and 450,000. My count was 1.4 million. Later I would learn what my doctors should already have known: a high platelet count is normally *not* a sign of CIDP. Dr. Kenton had handed my new physicians my diagnosis on a silver platter, but they refused to recognize it.

Bill and I now asked my doctors to revisit Dr. Kenton's diagnosis of POEMS syndrome. All three insisted they would, but explained that they still believed my symptoms were more closely associated with CIDP. I remember Bill specifically asking whether we shouldn't be taking a closer look at what he thought was my underlying problem: the bad "clone" of blood cells in my marrow that led to the high platelet count. The doctors explained that each patient was different, and each would experience some symptoms that were connected to their illness and others that were not. They wanted us to give the treatment I was currently receiving for CIDP—the Imuran, steroids and plasmapheresis—another six months, after which they would reevaluate my situation.

Six months? Did I have six months? I was nearly confined to a wheelchair, for God's sake!

At this point I was becoming thoroughly discouraged. My many blessings had been replaced with doubts and questions. What was happening to me? Would I ever get any answers? It was as though some strange force had decided to destroy me from the feet up.

How, I wondered, would it affect my family? And the question that haunted me the most: would I be forced to leave my career permanently? It was too agonizing to think about.

WHO ARE YOUR FRIENDS?

I wasn't quite awake when the phone rang. After a few seconds, I realized that no one else was going to answer it. Bill had already left for work, and Anna hadn't come in yet.

Reluctantly I picked up the receiver. It was a former colleague with whom I had worked for years. I sighed. I certainly didn't consider this person a friend. She liked to gossip too much, and I'd always thought her somewhat disingenuous.

"Hey, Leese. How ya feeling? I was just thinking about you; thought I'd call."

"I'm doing fair," I lied. "Seeing a little improvement, but at least I'm not regressing."

"So when do ya think you'll get back to work?'

"Oh, it'll be a while. I'm really focusing on my health right now. . . ."

"Ya know, I had a friend in California with mysterious symptoms . . . different from yours, but he also went to some of the best doctors in the country, had hundreds of sophisticated tests; he had been the picture of good health—and was dead in a year. Of course we know that won't happen to you."

"I sure hope not," I replied. "Asshole," I murmured under my breath.

"The procedure this guy had was something to do with . . ."

My thoughts began to drift away from the conversation. This was the type of acquaintance who thrived on other people's misfortunes and could run her mouth forever.

I interrupted her, "You know, someone's at my door. I'll have to talk with you later." I quickly hung up.

It is interesting how some people respond to you when you have a serious illness. With mine, I quickly learned who my true friends were, as Marianne Williamson shares so eloquently about friendship in her book *Illuminata*:

> True friendship reveals itself in time—not only in the sense of time spent together . . . , but also in the sense that it is through the ravages as well as the easier times in life that we come to see, as they say, "who are friends are."
>
> Loyalty to friends is easy when nothing rotten is in the air. But when rumors are flying, or innuendos, or betrayals—that is when the quality of true friendship becomes the stuff of heroic response. To give a friend the benefit of the doubt, to listen with depth and compassion and non-judgment to his story, . . . to be truly loyal in an age where loyalty is so easily relinquished—these are opportunities to use friendship as a means of righteous participation in life.
>
> We live at a time when people collect friends like we collect clothes—different types for different moods, seasonal, disposable. Friends should be like classics. . . . They should be a mainstay of life.

THOUGHTS AND HESITATIONS

My physical discomfort was fluctuating from hardly any at all to a deep and pulsating pain, emanating from the bone, from my calves down, along with a stinging, buzzing and burning sensation in my feet. A few months prior, the pain had reached only as high as my ankles, which had become weak and excruciatingly painful to the touch. I couldn't remember the last time I could move my toes more than slightly.

I could walk only from my house to my mailbox and back, about 20 yards, without feeling the need to rest. My power-walking days were long over. And I could lift only 10 pounds with my hamstrings. Three months earlier, I could easily press 30.

Looking back, I'm still disappointed and somewhat embarrassed that, as an educated, professional woman with access to the best medical facilities in the nation, I suffered nearly two years before my illness was accurately diagnosed. I thought my husband and I had asked all the right questions and had explored as many medical sources as we could for answers.

Despite the fact that we were not getting all the answers we wanted, we were initially hesitant to change doctors, thinking that the Lankenau hematologist, along with my neurologists at prestigious hospitals like Penn and Johns Hopkins, might be our best shot at getting to the bottom of my puzzling disorder, especially now that neurologist Heiman-Patterson at Hahnemann was at least looking more openly at POEMS syndrome.

Aside from Dr. Heiman-Patterson, Bill and I didn't always agree with the doctors, and we didn't really even like the other three, but we wanted to believe that they had my best interest at heart and that they were doing everything they could to make me well again. Surely, we thought, with them working together as a team, we had a better chance that one of them would notice something to either confirm that we were on the right track or show that we needed to move in a different direction.

CIDP AND OTHER AUTOIMMUNE DISEASES

With three of my four doctors believing strongly that I was suffering from CIDP, chronic inflammatory demyelinating polyneuropathy, I decided to find out everything I could about it and other autoimmune disorders.

Following months of research, I learned that almost all autoimmune illnesses can be quite puzzling. They develop when your immune system, which is designed to defend your body against disease, somehow identifies your healthy cells as foreign and attacks them.

Antibodies are proteins made by your immune system that help your body recognize and fight infections. When your antibodies are working properly, they target harmful substances, such as bacteria and viruses, by activating the immune system to get rid of them. However, when not operating the way they should, your antibodies can mistakenly target your healthy cells and tissue.

Imagine sailors on a ship; their mission is to protect their captain and fight a common enemy. But if something goes wrong, they may revolt. When you have an autoimmune disease, your antibodies stage a mutiny against your immune system by attacking those cells that they are supposed to protect.

In my case, my immune system perceived the myelin— the lining of my nerves—in my feet and legs as foreign and began attacking it. Myelin wraps around the nerve axon;

that's the long, wire-like part of a nerve cell. Myelin allows electrical impulses to travel efficiently along the nerve axon.

But when the myelin sheath is damaged, the electrical impulses are slowed or lost altogether, and those electrical impulses—the messages being transmitted—are disrupted. Some never make it to their final destination, thus the numbness, pain and other sensations in my legs and feet.

There are more than 80 types of autoimmune diseases, some of them extremely rare, and many with similar symptoms, making them difficult and frustrating to diagnose. Depending on the type, an autoimmune disease can affect one or various types of body tissue. It can also cause abnormal organ growth and changes in organ or muscle function.

Furthermore, there is no definitive cause for autoimmune diseases. What is known is that they tend to run in families, and that women, specifically African American, Hispanic and Native American women, have a higher risk for many of these ailments.

My mother, for much of her life, suffered with rheumatoid arthritis, an autoimmune disease that causes pain, swelling and stiffness in the joints. Her mother, my maternal grandmother, had Parkinson's disease, which many medical researchers suspect may be an autoimmune disease. Neurons in the brain are destroyed in Parkinson's disease. The cause is still unknown, but new studies have proposed that the neurons may be mistaken for foreign invaders and killed by the body's own immune system, similar to the way autoimmune diseases attack the body's cells.

Some doctors initially thought I had multiple sclerosis, a disease in which the immune system eats away at the protective myelin covering of the nerves, which was exactly what my disease was doing. MS is unpredictable and can be disabling; it's a disease of the central nervous system that disrupts the flow of information within the brain and between the brain and the body.

Other medical professionals thought I might be suffering from Guillain-Barré syndrome, which produces a tingling and weakness that begins in the extremities and often spreads from there. Some told me that my muscle weakness could evolve into paralysis. The most well-known outbreak of Guillain-Barré syndrome followed the mass vaccinations against the swine flu in the 1970s. It has also been studied as a possible result of the exposure to the herbicide Agent Orange, used in the Vietnam War.

Lupus was another autoimmune disorder that was considered when doctors first began trying to diagnose me. Lupus is an inflammatory disease, caused when the immune system attacks its own tissues. Various parts of the body can be affected, including the skin, joints and internal organs. Lupus can cause a wide variety of symptoms, some of which can be devastating.

My doctors had settled on CIDP, for the most part, Bill and I thought, because my major symptom and overwhelming problem at the time was chronic polyneuropathy. Yet this was only a *symptom*.

When doctors begin checking their patients for an autoimmune disease, they administer a test for antinuclear antibodies, ANAs, which attack healthy proteins in the nucleus or "brain" of your cells. While it is normal to have some antinuclear antibodies, having too many of these proteins will put you at an increased risk for developing an autoimmune disease.

A negative ANA test means that an active autoimmune disease is unlikely. And while a positive test can indicate that you have some type of autoimmune condition, it cannot diagnose you with a specific disorder. If your test comes back positive, your doctor will need to do more detailed testing to determine which autoimmune disease is causing your symptoms.

Besides the conditions already mentioned, other auto-immune illnesses associated with a positive ANA test are:

Scleroderma, a disease that causes the immune system to make too much of the protein collagen. As a result, the skin gets thick and tight, and scars can form on the lungs and kidneys.

Thyroid disease, which produces a range of symptoms that can affect the thyroid, including hypothyroidism and hyperthyroidism.

Type 1 diabetes, which develops when your immune system destroys cells known as beta cells in your pancreas; they're the ones that make insulin.

Alopecia areata, a type of hair loss that occurs when your immune system mistakenly attacks hair follicles, where the hair growth begins.

Addison's disease, an endocrine disorder in which the adrenal glands don't produce enough steroid hormones; usually this is due to damage to the adrenal gland by the body's own immune system.

Pernicious anemia, a condition in which a person's red blood cell count is low due to a deficiency of vitamin B_{12} or a protein called intrinsic factor that escorts B_{12} through the digestive system. The lack of sufficient intrinsic factor is often due to an autoimmune reaction in which a person's immune system mistakenly attacks the stomach cells that produce the factor.

Celiac disease, a disorder found in people who can't absorb nutrients properly. When they eat food

with gluten, their immune systems form antibodies to gluten, which then attack the lining of
the small intestine. Sufferers can end up mal-
nourished, no matter how much they eat.

Myasthenia gravis, a chronic autoimmune neuro-
muscular disease caused by a breakdown in
the normal communication between nerves
and muscles. Some symptoms are droopy eye-
lids; difficulties with speech, chewing and
swallowing; and weakness in arm and leg
muscles.

Sarcoidosis, the growth of tiny collections of
inflammatory cells called granulomas in different parts of the body, most commonly the lungs,
lymph nodes and skin. Many doctors believe this
disease results from the body's immune system,
but the mechanism is unknown. In about half
the cases of sarcoidosis, the symptoms go away
on their own. In other cases, the disease can last
for years and cause organ damage.

While most autoimmune diseases cannot be cured, many
doctors agree that the best diagnosis is likely to come from a
board-certified rheumatologist who specializes in these disorders. One such specialist, Dr. Anthony Albornoz, who is
affiliated with several hospitals in Delaware County, Pennsylvania, says there are multiple manifestations of the various autoimmune diseases. "Sometimes things appear not all
at once; you can have one feature of the autoimmune disease appear that may not be the most characteristic, and
then, a year later, all of the other symptoms or features will
appear. So it can be confusing. A good rheumatologist is
adept at being able to sort things out."

Therefore, there is no guarantee that even a specialist will be able to identify which of the many autoimmune disorders has stricken a particular patient, especially in the early stages of the disease. What we later learned was misleading my doctors was the polyneuropathy in my feet and legs. That autoimmune-like symptom was preventing them from seeing the bigger picture.

In my case, Bill and I thought that, if I didn't have CIDP but was instead suffering from some other autoimmune disorder with similar symptoms, it wasn't going to be easy finding the best treatment or a cure. What I learned later was that patients are commonly referred to a doctor who specializes in treating an early symptom of their disease. I suffered first from numbness, tingling and weakness in my feet and legs, so my husband sent me to a pair of neurologists. (The second neurologist, Dr. Kenton, did in fact accurately diagnosis my illness.) And because my illness involved a bad blood protein, I was referred to a hematologist. But it would eventually take the intervention of a gastroenterologist to see that I was being misdiagnosed and to get me to the doctor and the treatment that saved my life.

MORE SYMPTOMS, MORE DOCTORS

Just a couple of days after my final newscast in November 2003, my voice became progressively thinner. I found it increasingly more difficult to project my words. When friends or relatives came to visit, my voice became lost in the conversation.

Days later, my vocal quality was still raspy and feeble and was slowly worsening. I went to our ENT—our ear, nose and throat doctor—for testing. Dr. William Lewis first ordered a barium swallow, a test in which you drink a chalky liquid to coat your intestinal tract. An imaging machine then determines whether reflux may be causing problems with the vocal cords. My results confirmed I had a slight reflux but not enough to cause voice trouble.

Dr. Lewis then referred me to a well-known voice expert in Philadelphia, Dr. Joseph Sataloff, an otolaryngologist who worked with theatrical artists and opera singers worldwide. The practice, in an elegant 19th-century brownstone at 17th and Pine Streets, had been founded at the turn of the 20th century, and Dr. Sataloff had joined in 1946. When I visited him on a cool, breezy autumn afternoon, I was fascinated with both the man and the rich history of the medical practice. Sataloff's own work and research had improved the lives of tens of thousands of people with ear, nose and throat problems. He had saved the hearing of millions of American workers by forcing companies to purchase ear protectors and conduct ear tests. It was partly because of his tireless advocacy that the Occupational Safety and Health Administration (OSHA) was created.

Dr. Sataloff performed an ultrasound on my larynx and discovered that the nerves in my left vocal cord were paralyzed. Logically, I thought, he suspected POEMS. After all, the disease had destroyed the nerve linings in my feet and lower legs and had made its way to the tips of my fingers; why would it be surprising that it had traveled internally to my vocal cord?

Bill and I immediately contacted my doctors at Lankenau, Penn and Johns Hopkins with the news, and its probable relationship to my illness. Initially, they weren't sure what to make of the suggestion that somehow my disease was now affecting my ability to speak. Ultimately, each dismissed Dr. Sataloff's theory, suggesting that my vocal impairment was separate from and unrelated to my other problems, which they still suspected arose from CIDP.

I also contacted Dr. Terri Heiman-Patterson from Hahnemann about the news, and her response was that my disorder was looking more and more like POEMS. Since I was also having a few gastrointestinal issues, it appeared that nerves in my internal organs were now being attacked by the disease.

Dr. Heiman-Patterson had acknowledged the connection, and it was obvious to Dr. Sataloff, and to me and Bill, that whatever was causing my antibodies to attack the myelin in my feet and lower legs was now damaging my vocal cord. Dr. Sataloff prescribed voice rehab and physical therapy. He wanted to avoid surgery on my larynx, if at all possible.

WHERE DOES DEPRESSION HURT?

It was amazing how much my life had changed. I lay in bed most mornings, trying to muster the physical and emotional strength to get up. My husband had a new grip bar installed at waist height on our shower wall, and added a shower bench as well, but it still took me more than an hour to wash. My feet and ankles were severely rigid, my feet remained nearly numb on the bottoms and abnormally sensitive on the tops, and I could no longer move any of my toes.

Getting dressed was another real challenge. Pulling my socks on was the hardest part, and the tremor in my hands was so bad that simple tasks, like applying eyeliner or lipstick, were nearly impossible.

At this nadir in my life, I was forced to watch helplessly as clutter piled up around my house and many chores went unattended. It was all becoming an overwhelming task for me, and for Anna, my sitter/housekeeper. Yet I was so thankful for her, and she was thankful, I'm sure, that I had lost all concern for details and deadlines. I had been forced to release the reins—I was no longer in control.

Bill had been terrific, so patient, encouraging and supportive. He'd come home every day, after seeing patients at two offices and three hospitals, and check on me, prepare dinner, then help Lee with his homework. I remember feeling terribly guilty about having been a "bitch" on occasion. My medications, especially the prednisone, often caused me to lash out at him for no apparent reason. I was also overly sensitive about everything.

I knew I had developed a serious problem handling my health crisis when I became unable to project myself into the future. I struggled to get past the physical and emotional pain of my present. It appeared that "Dr. Prick" had been right about one thing. Mentally, I had sunk into a deep, dark hole.

"Where does depression hurt? Everywhere. Who does depression hurt? Everyone." Remember that TV commercial? I watched it describe vividly, over and over again, what I hated to admit, what I didn't want to accept. Hopelessness had begun to consume me.

I knew my husband loved me dearly and was desperately looking for answers. Bill and most of my family offered me endless support throughout my ordeal. Friends were there for me; thousands of Channel 6 viewers had sent me letters and cards. They had put me on their prayer lists at church and had masses said for me. Yet I felt empty and worthless.

CHAPTER SIX

WHERE DO I GO FROM HERE?

IT WAS MID-MARCH 2004 when Bill and I again discussed my visiting the Mayo Clinic in Rochester, Minnesota, as my gastroenterologist, Gary Newman, had suggested a few months earlier. I wasn't sure, however, that I was prepared to submit to the rigorous exams and evaluations that my research indicated I would undergo at Mayo. Furthermore, we had told my hematologist at Lankenau and neurologists at Penn and Johns Hopkins that we would give their treatment plan a few more months.

At this point in my illness, I was enduring more frequent episodes of such extreme nausea that I had to be hospitalized; sometimes this occurred as often as every six weeks. I would vomit until I became dehydrated and needed to receive fluids intravenously.

A TASTE OF
UNCONVENTIONAL MEDICINE

In the third week of March 2004, shortly after my latest hospital stay, I decided to investigate an unconventional treatment facility I had discovered in Marco Island, Florida. It was geared primarily toward cancer patients, promoting physical therapy and a radical change in diet as a cure for cancer and other diseases.

Bill, being a Western-taught physician, wasn't so sure about the unconventional part, but he thought it was a good idea for my mother to accompany me to Florida for a few weeks—if nothing else, for the sunshine and warm weather. It was the beginning of spring, but Philadelphia was still cold and damp, on the heels of an extra harsh winter. The plan was to have my sons come, too, for a week of their spring break.

The first week in Marco Island went okay; I wasn't feeling as well as I would have liked, but it was wonderful to be in a new environment. The Florida sunshine *can* cure a lot of ills, or at least make you feel as though it can. And the alternative diet wasn't as difficult an adjustment as I thought. Between meals of lentil soup, seaweed salad and cucumber juice, I had my colon cleansed and underwent reflexology therapy on my stiff and painful ankles and feet. Life felt at least tolerable, all things considered.

Then, without warning, I became violently ill. There's nothing worse than being rushed to an emergency room in a strange city where no one knows you. I admit I had been spoiled at Bryn Mawr Hospital back in the Philadelphia suburbs. There, I was recognized because of my position as a TV celebrity and my frequent ER visits, and I would often be preadmitted to the hospital. The most time I had spent in an emergency waiting room was about a half hour, and it was usually much less.

Here in Florida, doctors at the alternative care facility first gave me herbal, then organic antinausea medicine, but neither helped. They called an ambulance to take me to the nearest hospital in Naples. The trip took nearly an hour—a bumpy, tortuous ride in an old, beat-up ambulance. The paramedics were nice enough but had no authority to dispense any medication stronger than a Tylenol. They warned me to brace myself for at least another one-hour wait in the ER, but upon my arrival I realized I was in for a much more agonizing experience. Either there were an awful lot of really sick people coming to that hospital, I thought, or the emergency room nurses and doctors were the most indifferent and callous people on the planet.

I confess to having a rather low threshold for pain, but when I say I was sick, I am not exaggerating. I had severe stomach cramps and extreme nausea, which was beginning to turn into dry heaves, and no one even glanced in my direction. After the first hour of being ignored, I began to moan louder, just to get some attention. Several nurses actually looked at me with disgust.

Two hours passed, three, four, then finally after I threatened to lie on the floor and scream (my mother begged me not to do that), a nurse wheeled me into a cubicle to start an intravenous drip.

"I'm a tough stick, very small veins." I was barely able to talk.

"Well, let's see," said a petite woman with what appeared to be a permanent frown. She tried twice to thread a fat needle into my scrawny veins, with no luck.

"Don't you have a butterfly?" I asked, referring to the smaller needle typically used for tiny veins like mine.

"No, I'll get the IV team," said the woman.

"How long will that take?" my mother asked.

"Not long."

Ninety minutes later, a pudgy man with a partial smile came to my rescue. But by this time, my body wasn't even producing bile fast enough to replace what I would vomit. A hard-faced nurse snapped at me to stop sticking my fingers down my throat. "You're going to puncture your esophagus and then you'll have to go into emergency surgery," she warned.

All that did was frighten my mother, who begged me to stop, telling me I might die in that place, given the evidence of incompetence and indifference we had witnessed so far.

I was finally admitted to the hospital after more than six hours in the waiting area. But for the next six days, I suffered persistent nausea that, despite my being hydrated with IV fluids and given Zofran and Compazine, would not go away . . . until my seventh day. A male nurse, whose name I wish I could remember, had been kind to me, giving me ice chips and rubbing my back to relieve the nausea, even French-braiding my hair when it became excessively frizzy and tangled. Asking me about the narcotic Dilaudid that I was being prescribed for pain, he deduced that it might be what was causing my nausea. Sure enough, I was taken off Dilaudid at the nurse's suggestion, and I slept better that night than I had all week.

After six days of retching and writhing—feeling sicker for longer than I've ever felt—I awoke the next morning to a strange calmness. For a brief moment I thought perhaps it was death descending on me, but then I thought not, definitely not. This was different. It was a sense of peace, born of the realization that I was very much alive. I remember thinking I was in the arms of God.

The only times I could remember feeling something similar were my wedding day, July 12, 1980; the days my two sons were born, September 9, 1982, and August 9, 1985; and one night in the mid-1960s, an evening that certainly did not begin peacefully.

I was 11 years old. It was a domestic episode much like ones I would later report for Action News, but this one was happening at my own home. My dad had been on a drinking binge and was raging through our house, waving a pistol. In one senseless, terrifying moment, he fired into our coffee table, reducing part of it to splintered wood.

I was almost frozen with fear. My brothers—just Tim and Tom at the time; my mother was pregnant with Ted—cried and screamed for him to stop. But my mother was surprisingly serene throughout it all. I remember thinking how odd that was. After my father fired into the table, she simply asked him for the gun, and he handed it over.

I remember being unhappy with her reaction. I realize now that she was trying to be strong for her children, to let us know that everything would be okay, but at that moment I wanted her to respond with aggression. I wanted her to snatch the gun from that despicable crazy man and at least shoot him in the leg.

After the police carted my dad off to jail, my mother and brothers and I sat on the sofa holding each other, and I felt an inner peace. It was as though an aura of holiness was surrounding me, as though God had intervened to assure me that not only was I safe, but that the future was going to be bright.

In Naples Hospital, as I thought back to that traumatic night, I was drawn to the sun, which was shining brightly through my hospital window. I blinked repeatedly to clear my vision. In front of the window was my mother, asleep in the chair. She had been there all night.

⁓

Fortunately, my boys didn't arrive in Florida until after that first horrible week at Naples Hospital. Lee entered my hospital room with a high school football teammate, Justin Leake, and Lang came with his college girlfriend at the time, Sandra Cruz.

I had taken a much-needed shower beforehand, and the male nurse, my "terrestrial angel," braided my hair. He even added a little blush to my cheeks and applied a tinted gloss to brighten my lips.

I made an effort to sound upbeat and alert for my sons and their friends, but before they left to go back to their hotels, I could see the sadness in Lee's eyes. He is my sensitive child. He stayed behind for a few minutes and asked if I was sure I was okay. I tried to be as honest as I could. "I'm gonna be, Leland. I'm not feeling my best right now, but I'm going to be okay. I promise."

I firmly believed that I was going to get well, and Lee gave me a big hug.

The doctor at Naples conducted a test that I hadn't had before, a stomach-emptying test, which showed that I was digesting food much more slowly than I should have been. There was a 45% delay in the time it took my stomach to empty its contents—another sign, he and Bill and I thought, that whatever was attacking the lining of the nerves in my legs and had paralyzed one of my vocal cords was now launching an offensive on my digestive tract.

I stayed one more week at Naples Hospital before I was strong enough to return home, finally prepared to make a trip to the Mayo Clinic. An appointment with Dr. Angela Dispenzieri had been hastily arranged by Dr. Gary Newman. No postponements this time; Bill and I knew it was time to go.

HOME AGAIN, SICK AGAIN

Langston and Sandra had returned to Brown by the time I got back to Philadelphia. Leland was home, still on spring break. My first week home was uneventful.

By week two, I was back in the hospital.

The following is an entry from my journal, dated April 3, 2004:

> . . . bad, bad bad day! Not even two weeks home from Florida, had one of my "stomach things"—horrible gastrointestinal problem . . . threw up for 2 hours—got dehydrated, then induced myself to vomit the bile that remained, only to get a few minutes of relief before my retching started all over again . . . so hard for my mom and Bill to watch. I know they hate it when I stick my fingers down my throat, but I can't stop. It's hideous and humbling to the point of humiliation.

That night I went to Bryn Mawr Hospital near my home and stayed three days for IV fluids and more tests. It had now been more than five months since I left work a second time on medical leave. I had been pricked, poked, prodded and poked again. I'd had so many needles inserted into my arms and hands that I looked like a crack addict who'd been shooting up. I'd undergone numerous bone surveys, biopsies, bone marrow aspirations, nerve conduction studies, ENGs, EMGs, EKGs, X-rays, MRIs and many more tests. I was also taking about a dozen different medications and a myriad of supplements.

A "port" or catheter was implanted in my upper chest because I was regularly undergoing the procedure I mentioned earlier, plasmapheresis, in which my blood was withdrawn and then recycled back into my body after the bad plasma cells were removed and replaced with a synthetic albumin. It was a sickening procedure. I had endured it twice a week for six weeks. The plan had been to take a two-week break while I was in Florida and then go another six weeks.

I would have felt better about the ordeal if I'd thought it was even slightly working, but I had begun to feel weaker than ever, except when I got an occasional, superficial boost of energy from the prednisone. Given how my trip to Marco Island had ended, I could not have been happier about my upcoming visit to the Mayo Clinic. If only I could stay out of the hospital until then.

My biggest regret was that Leland had come with us that night I was admitted to Bryn Mawr Hospital. The following is what he later wrote about my illness; it provided a haunting insight into the impact my illness had had on hir

First, you should know that growing up with my mom being a local celebrity was exciting. It could also sometimes be surreal. To me, it seemed that just about everyone knew who she was, could recall a time and place that they had run into her and tell me a story reflective of how kind and genuine she is "in person." It was as if they all thought I didn't know my mom was Superwoman; that she was extraordinary.

I knew.

Growing up, there was nothing my mom couldn't do—no task too big, no childhood disappointment too small or undeserving of her immediate attention. She was there every morning to make sure I ate a good breakfast—pancakes, eggs and bacon, with a tall glass of ice cold milk, were usually on the menu. And, until my older brother got his driver's license, it was also mom who drove us to school every morning, before getting herself ready for work.

This is how things went throughout my childhood and into my teenage years; my superhero mom was always there for me, and Lisa Thomas-Laury was always there for Philadelphia.

I didn't mind sharing her.

In 2002, however, this all changed . . . my worst nightmare became a reality. Suddenly, I realized my mom was human. She became seriously ill, and no one seemed to know what was wrong with her—not even my other hero, my dad, who is a doctor.

It was a tough time for me. It left me feeling distraught, and lost.

On the outside, I refused to give in to what I was going through, or what we were going through as a family. I fought hard not to show any emotion when asked how my mom was doing—it didn't matter whether you were a relative or a friend—"Thank you for asking. She's doing better." And if anyone, God forbid, asked how I was dealing with everything . . . I always simply replied, "OK."

For too many years, I was neither ready nor willing to show emotion or speak openly about my mom's illness.

It was when I was alone that my thoughts would race, and I would struggle to cope with my personal anguish; how could this happen? When will she get better? Is she going to get better? What can I do to fix it? For some reason I neglected to ask my dad or her doctors any of these questions, perhaps for fear I wouldn't be able to handle the answers . . .

CHAPTER SEVEN

MAYO, HERE
I COME

I ARRIVED IN Rochester, Minnesota, in mid-April 2004. I was still feeling some effects from my last hospital stay at Bryn Mawr, but I was excited about my visit with Dr. Dispenzieri. First, however, I was going to be poked and prodded again for several days.

It had been suggested that Bill and I stay at the Holiday Inn by Marriott, which was attached to the Mayo Clinic. This was a good choice. All Bill and I had to do was take the elevator to the subway level, and we were just a few yards from most of my medical appointments.

WHAT A DIFFERENCE
A HOSPITAL MAKES

My first impression of the Mayo Clinic was how huge it was. Even more surprising was how genuinely nice everyone was. And I do mean everyone . . . nurses, doctors, technicians, janitors, shop owners, everyone!

As sick and weak as I was, this place made me smile.

It was a Tuesday morning, 6:45 a.m., and I had a full four-day schedule of every test you could imagine. Bill and I set out, with him pushing me in my wheelchair.

First, blood work in the Hilton Building, subway level. I was to report to Desk C. The Hilton Building was the farthest away, and Bill pushed me the whole distance, as I had become too weak to walk even with my leg braces.

Ten minutes, and I was called to Door A for my blood test. A friendly young woman named Laurie asked me which arm offered the most success in drawing blood. I explained that my veins were small and often rolled, but suggested she try my right arm. I added that I hadn't been able to drink a lot of fluids because of other tests scheduled that day. Smiling, she assured me it would be okay. The next thing I knew she was filling a fifth vial with my blood. I had felt only the tiniest pinch. At the first stick, my blood was flowing freely through the narrow tube into one vial after another—12 of them in all.

7:00 a.m.: specimen collection. I obtained a three-liter, amber-colored container with a handle at Desk A to collect my urine for 72 hours.

8:00 a.m.: I reported to the Gonda Building, sixth floor, Desk 6 South, for an echocardiogram, an ultrasound of my heart. It would provide Dr. Dispenzieri with information about the size of my heart, how well it was pumping and how the valves were working.

9:30 a.m.: Same building, 10th floor, an electrocardiogram (EKG) to check for any problems with my heart's electrical activity.

11:00 a.m.: Charlton Building, Nuclear Medicine section, back the opposite way through the Mayo Atrium, past the entrance to my hotel. I reported to the first floor, Desk 1, for a PET scan. Positron emission tomography (PET) is an imaging test that uses a special dye injected into a vein in your arm. The dye contains radioactive tracers that are absorbed by organs and tissues in your body. Doctors can often detect the early onset of a disease with a PET scan, before it becomes evident on other imaging tests.

My next examination was scheduled for 1:30 p.m., after time for a little lunch in the Mayo Cafeteria or snack in the gift shop, if my next test would allow. As it turned out, my next exam was a pulmonary function test (PFT), back at the Gonda Building, 18th floor, Desk 18 East, and it *would* permit me a light snack beforehand. The Mayo Clinic functions like a well-oiled machine. Every detail is considered, and the timing of my appointments was spot on.

The PFT provided my doctor with important information about how much air my lungs could hold. It measured the amount of airflow into and out of my lungs and analyzed the transfer of oxygen and other gases between lungs and bloodstream.

3:15 p.m.: My final examination that Tuesday afternoon was a bone marrow biopsy, again at the Gonda Building, seventh floor, Desk 7E. During this procedure I required IV sedation. First, a marrow aspiration was performed to obtain a sample of the liquid portion of my bone marrow. Next, a syringe with a larger needle was used to withdraw a small sample of solid bone marrow tissue. Despite what some people think, the procedure is not painful, not even when the anesthesia wears off. That site in your back might be just a little sore.

The following three days also began around 7:00 a.m., with examinations stretching until 3:30–4:00 p.m. At last, on Friday, I ended the day with a 3:30 meeting with the doctor I was now quite eager to meet.

Dr. Dispenzieri entered the exam room with a big smile on her face, which helped tremendously to put Bill and me at ease. I noticed she was wearing little if any makeup, and her hair was slightly disheveled. She looked as though she had been busy all day, and I supposed she had not gone out for lunch, most likely eating a sandwich or yogurt and fruit in her office.

She got right to the point.

A FAMILIAR AND
FRIGHTENING DIAGNOSIS

"You have POEMS syndrome," said Dr. Dispenzieri, rather matter-of-factly. "You've had it all along. It is shutting you down. I'm recommending a stem cell transplant, but you're too weak now. We will send you home, build you up a little, and then you'll come back in a few months for the procedure."

Bill and I were both stunned and relieved. POEMS! Finally I had an accurate diagnosis.

We never doubted this "wonder woman," as we called her, so confident were we in what she had discovered about my health crisis. After all, it's what we had suspected, albeit on and off, from the beginning. And I had undergone nearly two dozen tests and exams at one of the top medical facilities in the world. My treating doctor had written the standard of care for POEMS syndrome. Also, she didn't say I *think* you have POEMS, or *all indications are* that you have POEMS. She said, "You *have* POEMS syndrome. You've had it all along."

It took us a few minutes to process what Dr. Dispenzieri had told us. We both had lots of questions, and she took all the time needed to answer them, though she was careful not to malign our other physicians when we asked how they could have been so wrong, how they could have misdiagnosed the illness for so long.

Later, I found there was one thing Dr. Dispenzieri had mentioned that I couldn't get out of my head. "It is shutting you down," she'd said.

"Was she saying what I thought?" I asked Bill.

At first he didn't answer.

"Honey," I asked more directly, "when the doctor said this thing was shutting me down, she meant it was killing me, right?"

"No," Bill replied, "she was talking about the parts of your body it has already impacted."

I accepted his answer, but I thought about all the parts of my body that had already been damaged by the illness: the nerves in my feet and lower legs (I could no longer walk the short distance across my kitchen or stand without support for even five minutes); the grip and strength in my hands (I couldn't open a new jar of pickles or sew a button on a sweater); my penmanship (because of the tremor in my hands, my handwriting resembled the shaky strokes of my maternal grandmother when she was suffering from Parkinson's disease); my eyesight (the LASIK surgery I'd had a few years earlier, which allowed me to read the teleprompter without contacts, was no longer effective); my voice (I could no longer project it the way I used to, and my left vocal cord was paralyzed).

In addition to all this, the doctors in Florida had deduced, and Dr. Dispenzieri agreed, that I was suffering from gastroparesis, a condition that delays the time it takes for the stomach to empty food into the small intestine. The vagus nerve, which controls the muscles in the stomach, had been damaged.

I knew the answer to my question; I knew the truth, I just couldn't bring myself to acknowledge it. When we returned to our hotel, I immediately went to my computer and looked up the phrase "shut down" in the online dictionary and thesaurus: *the act of stopping the operation of . . . for a period of time or forever; to terminate or expire, close, end, discontinue, kill.*

Hell, no! Not me, I told myself.

As it turned out, my pulmonary function test had shown that I had severe respiratory insufficiency, which, Dr. Dispenzieri explained, meant I wasn't strong enough to undergo a bone marrow transplant at the time. She said she was sending us home with some daily respiratory exercises to improve pulmonary function capacity, plus a new diet to build up nutrients in my body.

I was more optimistic than ever. And on a mission to get well again!

CHAPTER EIGHT

POEMS, NO RHYME
OR REASON

At that meeting in her office, Dr. D, as I soon began to think of her, told Bill and me that, yes, doctors should have been attacking my underlying problem, the blood aspect of my illness, my protein imbalance. A stem cell transplant, she told us, would obliterate my abnormal cell clone (the very question Bill had asked the Johns Hopkins neurologist and Lankenau hematologist repeatedly) and give me a very good chance of recovery.

Furthermore, she confirmed that my polyneuropathy, my abnormal protein, my excessively high platelet count, the changes in my skin pigmentation and the sclerotic lesions found on my femur and hip bone in the skeletal survey performed at Mayo—all these were concrete signs of POEMS syndrome.

Plasmapheresis and IVIG were never beneficial treatments for me, she shared. Neither was the drug Imuran, which she stopped on the spot. Dr. D agreed that the paralysis in my vocal cord was due to POEMS and that my gastroparesis was at least consistent with POEMS.

Now that Bill and I knew for sure that I'd had POEMS all along, I wanted to know even more about this ugly and enigmatic illness. What *was* POEMS syndrome?

The disorder was first described by a Dr. Crow in Britain in 1956, and then by a Dr. Fukase in Japan in 1968. It was dubbed Crow-Fukase syndrome, a name by which it is still sometimes known. Researchers also say POEMS is slightly more prevalent among men than women. The average age for the onset of the illness is 48 for men and 59 for women. However, the disorder has been reported in patients as young as 15.

As I mentioned back in Chapter 3, "POEMS" is an acronym that highlights the most significant symptoms of the disorder. After my visit to Dr. D, I began exploring its meaning in more detail.

P = Polyneuropathy

In many cases the first symptom of POEMS syndrome involves the peripheral nervous system, which consists of all the motor and sensory nerves that connect the brain and spinal cord to the rest of the body. Sufferers experience weakness, pain, numbness and/or a tingling-like sensation, beginning in their feet and legs, with their symptoms progressively working their way upward. A bilateral peripheral neuropathy most often affects the feet and legs, but as time progresses the hands may also become affected. This neuropathy is why the disorder is so commonly mistaken for CIDP.

O = Organomegaly

About two-thirds of patients with POEMS will develop an abnormally enlarged liver; one-third of patients will have an abnormally enlarged spleen, and some will exhibit swollen lymph nodes. A biopsy of the lymph nodes may show Castleman's disease, itself a rare and vicious immune disorder.

E = Endocrinopathy

Men and women with POEMS can exhibit various abnormalities affecting the endocrine system, the system of glands that secrete hormones into the blood system. Men may experience erectile dysfunction or impotence, or an abnormal enlargement of their breasts. Women may see their menstrual cycles stop, or even an abnormal discharge of milk from their nipples. Some women may experience an overproduction of estrogen and an increased libido.

M = Monoclonal gammopathy

Monoclonal gammopathies, also known as plasma cell dyscrasias, are a group of disorders characterized by the uncontrolled growth of a single clone (hence the term "monoclonal") of a certain type of plasma cell. An overproduction of plasma cells can lead to the formation of masses, or tumors, consisting of plasma cells, that appear like scars, or sclerotic lesions, on a bone X-ray.

In most cases, the specific type of plasma cell dyscrasia associated with POEMS syndrome is osteosclerotic myeloma, which is a variant of multiple myeloma. Some doctors refer to POEMS as a "smoldering" myeloma.

S = Skin abnormalities

A variety of skin irregularities may be present in patients with POEMS syndrome, including an abnormal darkening of the skin, which is known as hyperpigmentation, or a "dusky" appearance of the feet and ankles; a hardening and thickening of the skin (sclerosis); excessive sweating (hyperhidrosis); and excessive hair growth (hypertrichosis).

Other symptoms often associated with POEMS syndrome are increased levels of platelets, responsible for clotting in the blood, and abnormally high levels of vascular endothelial growth factor (VEGF) in the serum.

POEMS syndrome was originally thought to be more common in Japan than the United States or Europe, but the disorder is often misdiagnosed, making it difficult to determine its true frequency. "No matter how you slice it, it's rare," said Dr. D. "But I think there are many more patients with POEMS than what we give it credit for."

Chronic inflammatory demyelinating polyneuropathy, or CIDP, is most often the disease for which POEMS is mistaken. "That's the great mimic," Dr. D told us. "That's the look-alike. There are simple things, like high platelet count, you don't see that in CIDP, and you see that in about half of all patients with POEMS. So, for the doctor . . . that should be a little aha moment."

Did she think that, like mesothelioma, the rare, aggressive cancer caused by asbestos, my rare, precancerous POEMS syndrome may have been caused by exposure to chemicals produced at the Union Carbide plant near my home? "That's what the whole field of epidemiology is about. . . . There are so many diseases, and we don't know why they develop . . . but [with POEMS] I think we know more about the overall prognosis."

The prognosis for mesothelioma patients is usually poor. Symptoms often lie latent in people who have worked with, or been exposed to, asbestos, and they can take 20–50 years to appear. I asked Dr. D whether the same may be true of POEMS. "It is certainly possible," she said.

In the 1960s and 1970s, studies showed a disproportionate number of cancer and suicide cases in Institute, Dunbar, Charleston and other towns surrounding the chemical plants where I grew up. And an unusually high number of mesothelioma cancer deaths were also linked to exposure to asbestos among plant workers in Institute and Nitro, West Virginia.

⌒

In two months and one week, I was ready to make a second trip to the Mayo Clinic for my bone marrow transplant. Coincidentally, around this same time I got a call from Todd MacCulloch, the former Sixers center, who was also thought to have CIDP. He called to tell me that Dr. Terry Heiman-Patterson had determined that he was actually suffering from Charcot-Marie-Tooth disease, a hereditary disorder that damages the nerves in the arms, legs and feet. Apparently, his mother had come to visit him, and she had been suffering similar symptoms. When the doctor saw her, she figured it out.

CHAPTER NINE

MARVELOUS MAYO

In mid-July 2004, just before my 50th birthday, I returned to the Mayo Clinic in Rochester for the stem cell transplant. It had been decided that I would undergo an autologous transplant, meaning I would be both the recipient and the donor—that is, my own stem cells would be used. Dr. Dispenzieri told me that I had enough "good" bone marrow to harvest and use in my own treatment, and that I even had enough suitable marrow to freeze and store for any future transplants I might require. I wouldn't need to have relatives tested to determine who might be a match.

The plan was for my mother to travel with me this time, and for each of my three brothers and my sister-in-law to come for a long weekend to assist my mom following my transplant. Bill would be holding down the fort at home with our younger son, Lee, now a high school graduate, who was preparing to enroll at the University of Virginia in Charlottesville. His brother, Lang, was staying in Providence for the summer, taking some extra classes at Brown.

Although I was doing better with my leg braces on occasion, my mom's rheumatoid arthritis prevented her from pushing me for even short distances in a wheelchair. To help us get around, she and I rented motorized scooters. Because I had a caregiver with me, I wouldn't be required to stay in the hospital for an extended period. At Mayo most stem cell transplants are conducted as outpatient procedures. Overall, though, I would be staying in Rochester for at least two months before I'd be well enough to return home.

OUTPATIENT HOUSING

With Bebe—the boys' name for their grandma, which all of us had adopted—I had looked at several housing possibilities. Sunny Place Cottage, within the Serenity House Network, offered a two-bedroom, one-bath private home exclusively for Mayo Clinic patients, their families and caregivers. It was located within 10 minutes of the Mayo campus, and the price was reasonable: $79.00 per night for a 30-day stay.

The Nazarene Well House was another great choice for an even lower price. A bed-and-breakfast-style accommodation for patients and their families during treatment, the Well House is a large residential home with 13 bedrooms (five with private baths), a well-equipped kitchen and off-street parking. A continental breakfast is donated by a local bakery, and a local Italian restaurant donates some dinners. There are also two on-site caretakers. There was a waiting list when I was at Mayo, partly because the cost was an extremely inexpensive $30.00 per night.

There were numerous other group homes and charitable lodging possibilities for Mayo Clinic patients, but when I realized I'd had unused reward points from the Marriott Hotel since the 1980s, I decided to use them for a two-bedroom suite at the Holiday Inn by Marriott, where Bill and I had stayed during my first visit to Rochester. Each of the bedrooms there had its own bath, so my mother could have her privacy during our extended stay. In addition, our suite had a sofa bed in the main room for other family members, plus a well-stocked kitchenette with a full-sized-fridge, stove, oven and microwave. It was also connected to the Mayo Clinic via the subway level, which made it especially easy for Bebe and I to make our way around on our motorized scooters. There would be no need to even go outside unless we chose to.

MAYO ART AND DESIGN

That first week of my return to Mayo, I asked myself how I had failed to appreciate the magnificence and beauty of the facility. The entrance lobby at the Gonda Building has one of the most beautiful atriums you'll ever see. Adorned with Brazilian granite and marble from all over the world, the Nathan Landrum Atrium appears to be in unique congruity with the design of the adjacent Mayo and Charlton buildings. All three are linked physically by skyways and a sweeping wave wall of glass.

On the back wall of the atrium is a giant sculpture of a man wearing only a fig leaf and looking upward, with his arms and hands reaching upward as well. Many Christians view this work by sculptor Ivan Meštrović as an image of Jesus. The 6900-pound cast bronze sculpture is entitled *Man and Freedom*. According to information kept by a former Mayo Clinic administrator, the late Robert Roessler, the sculpture has special meaning at Mayo. Roessler and others thought it was rightly named for its home, because thousands at the Mayo Clinic continue to work for man's freedom from health issues.

In the long hallway leading from the subway elevator to the Holiday Inn and the Charlton Building is a series of large, colorful animal paintings, Andy Warhol's *Endangered Species*. In the lobby of the Rochester Methodist Hospital, part of the Mayo complex, is a fantastically carved mother-of-pearl box donated by King Hussein and Queen Noor of Jordan. Saudi Arabia's royal family has also been known to gift the Mayo Clinic with large monetary donations and artifacts, in gratitude for medical care received.

We heard that the Saudis made frequent visits—a claim we'd have occasion to confirm for ourselves.

Mayo has an extensive collection of glass, china and pottery as well. Our favorites were the 13 Chihuly chandeliers, a marvelous array of multicolored hand-blown glass pieces, some with elongated cylindrical forms, others more global. You can look up and view them from the subway level, or go to the Mayo Nurses Atrium on the first floor and see them more closely. They are the creations of American glassblower Dale Chihuly, considered the world's foremost glass master, and they are made much like the beautiful items in the famous Murano glass factory in Venice, Italy.

The timeless works of Rodin, Warhol and other renowned artists are also found throughout the Mayo Clinic buildings. It is said, in fact, that the original founders of the clinic, William and Charles Mayo, wanted to use art and architecture to address the "spiritual aspects" of medical care. And indeed, looking at all the surrounding beauty as you make your way to and from your appointments, there is no doubt your spirits are lifted.

THE TRANSPLANT PROCESS

However beautiful and interesting the clinic proved to be, my transplant was a long and complicated process.

First there was a conditioning regimen, a series of tests and examinations to assess my overall level of health. That first week at Mayo, I had:

+ An echocardiogram to assess the function and structure of my heart and nearby blood vessels.
+ An electrocardiogram to check my heart's rhythm and electrical activity.

+ An X-ray and computed tomography (CT) scan to check the condition of organs such as lungs and liver.
+ Various blood tests to check the level of blood cells and assess how well the liver and kidneys were working.
+ Pulmonary tests to determine how well my lungs were functioning.

Next, before doctors could perform my transplant, they had to harvest some of my "good" bone marrow. Unlike what many people think of bone marrow transplants and harvesting, there is no real pain; it can all be done through the blood. The most common way to harvest stem cells involves temporarily removing blood from the body, separating the stem cells from the blood, and then returning the blood to the body. It's done with a special cell-separator machine.

First, I received a medication to increase the number of stem cells in my blood. I took this medicine for four days prior to the transplant. On the fifth day, a blood test determined that I had enough circulating stem cells.

Next, veins in both of my arms were connected by tubes to the cell-separator machine. Blood was then removed from one arm and passed through a filter before being returned to my body through the other arm. Not at all painful, the procedure was done while I was fully awake. It took about four hours.

Next, I received a mega-dose of the strongest chemotherapy to destroy any existing bone marrow cells and make room for the transplanted tissue. I received melphalan, which, along with cyclophosphamide, is commonly used for this purpose. The drug would also destroy any existing precancerous or cancerous cells and shut down my immune system to reduce the risk of my transplant's being rejected.

The bone marrow transplant itself is usually done the day after your "good" marrow is harvested. In my case, a central venous catheter or "port" had been inserted in my neck, into a vein near my heart, so that I could receive the necessary medicines without the need for repeated injections. The marrow was delivered back into my bloodstream through that port.

The process is similar to getting a blood transfusion. The stem cells travel through the blood into the bone marrow. It took just a few hours.

Stem cell transplants can have some unpleasant side effects, though, especially during the conditioning phase. I suffered severe fatigue and nausea, as well as hair loss caused by the chemotherapy. But it helped tremendously to have my mother with me, and my other caregivers who arrived weekly to offer support.

I remember vividly the morning I awoke to find large clumps of hair on my pillow. My oldest brother, Tom, was visiting at the time, and he offered to shave my head. Despite my initial concern, it was liberating. It released me from all the fears and inhibitions that had piled up inside me since the onset of my illness. Plus, I was relieved that I had a rather nicely shaped noggin.

A CULTURAL ENCOUNTER

Remember that I mentioned the Saudi royal family? Midway through my stay at Mayo, Saudi Arabia's Crown Prince Abdullah arrived in Rochester in his private jet, along with four wives, several ex-wives and 30-plus sons and daughters, all for medical checkups. Traveling with them were dozens of other members of his entourage, including a team of chefs and assistants. The Crown Prince and his current wives checked into the penthouse atop the Kahler Grand Hotel, also connected to the clinic, for nearly one month. The remainder of his party filled five floors of the four-star hotel.

I didn't encounter the Crown Prince himself during our stay in Rochester, but there was lots of talk among the Mayo staff, and some patients, about the 747SP jet from Saudi Arabia landing at Rochester's tiny airport. The aircraft, we were told, seated as many as 400 people on two passenger levels. An article in a Rochester newspaper estimated that approximately 200 people connected to the royal family had arrived in the city. There was excitement not only because of curiosity about the culture, but also because the Saudis were known to be extravagant shoppers. A conservative estimate of the royal family's spending during a previous visit to Rochester had reached $1.5 million.

Just a few days after word of the royal family's arrival, a Mayo nurse told me and JaNeen, my sister-in-law (the second caregiver to travel to Rochester following my brother Tom), that her daughter had spotted a fleet of high-end luxury cars, along with five U-Hauls, parked outside the Apache Mall. One of the cleaning ladies at our hotel said she had spotted three very nice vehicles with tinted windows and New York plates outside a nearby Walmart. Turns out that they, too, were part of the Saudi contingency, and she had taken pictures of the people getting into the cars.

Days later, JaNeen, or Neeny as we call her, suggested that if I was feeling well enough, we should get out of the hotel for an hour or so. Thankfully, I was no longer sleeping most of the day, and Neeny encouraged me to go with her to visit some boutiques and stores, including a frozen yogurt shop she had discovered in the subway level of the Kahler Hotel. She knew that frozen yogurt and milkshakes were about all I felt up to eating at the time, so I agreed. Just a few minutes into our outing, we spotted a group of young girls, teenagers, dressed in their native abayas (long cloaks or robe-like dresses) and head scarves. They were visiting a nail salon two doors down from the yogurt shop. Suspecting that they were part of the royal family, and keenly curious, Neeny and I headed their way. None of the girls had on any makeup, which we knew their culture discouraged, so we were surprised they were getting manicures.

I noticed that the girls appeared to be especially impressed with JaNeen, who was wearing shorts, a short-sleeved top and flip-flops. To almost anyone in America, she was dressed appropriately for a hot day in August. She was wearing little makeup, only a peach lipstick. But she must have been a marvel to the young Arabians. I was wearing jeans, a long-sleeve top and tennis shoes, as I was excessively cold post-transplant. I was also sporting my medical mask, which was required while my immune system remained compromised, and a baseball cap. My attire covered almost as much of me as did the clothing of the young foreign visitors.

I should also mention that my sister-in-law's family is from Trinidad. She is a beautiful, petite young woman with flawless light-mocha-colored skin and long flowing dark hair. No doubt, the young Saudi girls were in awe of Neeny, who resembled them but was dressed in Western attire that men in their culture would find much too revealing.

Neeny and I decided to get our nails done as well, and she landed a manicurist and seat next to one of the Saudi teens. The seats were close enough that you could easily strike up a conversation, and sure enough, in a matter of minutes, I noticed that JaNeen was engaged in a seemingly delightful conversation with the young Saudi girl beside her. I was seated next to a woman from Wisconsin whose husband was undergoing a heart transplant, and while her story and our conversation were thoroughly fascinating, I couldn't wait to find out what Neeny had discussed with the giggly, fully clothed girl to her right.

And Neeny couldn't wait to tell me.

"Oh my God, Lisa, wait till you hear what she asked me."

"What?" I said as we walked out of the salon.

"Her name is Amal. She was very shy at first; I initiated the conversation, asking her where she was from, when she arrived and things like that . . . then I told her that I thought her culture was so interesting. She would say only that she agreed with me, and that she also thought American culture was intriguing. I thought she might say that hers was too restrictive, but it seemed that she was not going to say anything bad."

"Did she say anything about being allowed to wear makeup or get her nails done?" I asked eagerly.

"Yes, yes! I told her that I was surprised she was getting her nails done, and she said they were allowed to, but only when they traveled to the U.S., and that they could only get a clear polish or a French manicure, no color! Then she didn't say much for a while, then guess what?"

"What?" I asked impatiently.

"She asked me if I was allowed to choose my own husband."

"Get out!" I exclaimed.

We couldn't wait to tell Bebe. And the three of us would talk throughout the weekend about our surprise encounter with the girls from Saudi Arabia. We were so physically close to them that day, yet so many miles apart in our lifestyles.

THE SCOOTER GIRLS

During her four-day stay, Neeny dubbed my mom and me "the scooter girls" as we made our way to and from my appointments on our motorized scooters. Fortunately for us, Neeny was able to turn an annoying problem into a situation that we found hysterically entertaining.

When we traveled on our scooters, I would often stop either to recheck our destination or to admire a piece of art or other item in a store window. While I would always raise my left hand to alert my mother that I was going to hit the brake—as we both had learned long ago in driving school—she would, without fail, rear-end me. More often than not, it would be a jolting bump, and I was irritated.

Initially, this was amusing only to JaNeen. Later, though, Bebe and I became so tickled at Neeny's response that we found ourselves cracking up at each come-from-behind collision. It got to the point that, when one of us recalled our motor scooter bang-ups, we all dissolved into laughter.

FAMILY MATTERS

The week before he was to move into his dorm at the University of Virginia, Lee begged his dad to let him visit me in Rochester. Those were a wonderful three days in which Lee, Bebe and I watched movies together, talked and listened to Lee tell us stories about his summer. Lee is a great storyteller. And my baby boy was also quick to comfort me on a day when I wasn't feeling so well. When I expressed regret that I couldn't be there for his college move-in, he didn't hesitate to assure me that he would be just fine.

As it turned out, God answered my prayers, and Lee's first year at UVA went remarkably well. He loved the school and had a terrific first-year roommate, a Virginia native, Alex Annear, who played the trumpet in the university band and collected all types of music. Though Alex is white, he introduced his new African American friend to the marvels of Motown. Imagine how hard I laughed when Lee called me in Rochester to ask whether I'd ever heard of this incredible singer named Marvin Gaye, and a song he recorded called "What's Going On."

My younger son had long ago forgotten the old-school tunes Bill and I had played at our parties, especially outside at our pool on hot summer nights: songs by performers like Earth, Wind & Fire, the Temptations, Otis Redding, Al Green, the Stylistics and the Delfonics. So Alex Annear introduced my little rap enthusiast to a cacophony of new soulful sounds, an entire new world of melodies. And Alex's mother, Sarah, knowing that I was going through some health issues, sent me a lovely UVA tree ornament for Christmas. Lee made other lifelong friends that first year in Charlottesville and managed to earn a B average in his classes.

I was also in touch regularly with my older son, Langston, during my transplant ordeal. He had moved off campus to rent a house with some friends at Brown during his third year, and he was still there taking summer classes. Except for the excessive number of parking tickets accumulating in the back seat of Lang's car, I wasn't too worried about him.

Along with my oldest brother, Tom, my younger brothers, Tim and Ted, also spent time with Bebe and me in Rochester during my post-transplant recovery. Ted, the youngest, was more like an infant son when we were kids.

Nearly 12 years older, I was thrilled to have my own little live baby doll to take care of. And I had lots of mommy duties with "Teddy boo" when he was little. I loved to tease him whenever he got on my nerves as an adult, reminding him that I had once changed his diapers. That would almost always nip his annoying behavior in the bud.

However, I had a chance at Mayo to see my baby bro from an entirely new perspective. He and JaNeen had met about a year after he left Institute to live with our brother Tom in Dallas. I had already been working for almost a decade in Philadelphia by then. Ted graduated from the University of Texas at Dallas in 1989, got a job with Federal Express, and met JaNeen when he was 21 and she was only 16 years old.

I marveled at how much he had matured. After all, this was the kid who would mischievously spy on my high school boyfriend Harvey and me when we cuddled on the front porch, and he would streak past us, butt-naked, at the most inopportune times. Ted had his own son now, Jordan, and it was immensely gratifying to see what a wonderful father he had become.

For my middle brother, Tim, always the quiet and reserved sibling, the visit to Rochester was an opportunity for him and Bebe to have some one-on-one time. I was initially disappointed that he didn't seem interested in what I was going through and that he didn't make more time to talk with me. Afterwards, I realized that as president of the Art Institute in New York City, Tim had been dealing with terrible stress. In addition, he and his wife, Randi, hoping to adopt a child from China, had been put on a long waiting list. They knew it could take more than a year. Tim had also been experiencing severe back pain for several months.

Furthermore, it was good for my mom to have something else to focus on besides me and my illness. She wanted to be there for all of her children, and it would have been selfish of me to interfere with that.

Before Tim left, he, Bebe and I held hands over my bed, and he said a heartfelt prayer for me and our mother: that I would continue improving from my transplant, and that God would give Bebe the strength to continue watching over and comforting me.

A LONG RECOVERY

I continued to improve, but it was a slow process. Though not in much pain, I was still extremely fragile. In the first few weeks following my stem cell transplant, it took all of my energy each morning just to get out of bed, go to the bathroom, brush my teeth and walk to the main room of our suite to sit or lie on the sofa.

Having dropped about 36 pounds, I had explicit instructions from a Mayo dietician to try to eat 1200 calories per day at first, then at least 1500 to 1800, with an emphasis on a diet high in calcium and phosphorus to strengthen my bones. That was much more difficult than it sounded, because I had lost interest in most foods. My doctor assured me that was normal and encouraged me to consume as many milkshakes as I wanted, along with yogurt, puddings, creamed soup and cheese.

Fortunately, one of the restaurants in Rochester that delivered to our hotel was Victoria's, which had the best pasta dishes. As soon as my appetite began to creep back, I would order the Mushroom Passion Crab Ravioli. To die for! The portions at Victoria's are generous, and when I started ordering this dish I'd have enough for three days. By the time

I was four weeks post-transplant, I'd order and eat a whole serving at least twice a week.

Gradually, over the next two months at Mayo, I began to regain my strength. I started to gain weight, my pulmonary capacity began to improve and my platelet levels were declining. I was still rather weak, but I began to do some light cardio exercises and weight lifting in the hotel gym. I knew as soon as I returned home and began a consistent exercise regimen, I would start feeling like my old self again. However, Dr. Dispenzieri suggested that I wait at least a year before returning to WPVI-TV.

CHAPTER TEN

THE STRUGGLE
TO RETURN
TO WORK

ONE YEAR and two months after my transplant, my Channel 6 news director and general manager, Carla Carpenter and Dave Davis, were eager for me to return to work. But something was holding me back.

I couldn't quite come to grips with my ambivalence about resuming my career. I loved what I did for a living. It was what I had always dreamed of doing. However, I had seen TV news from a different perspective since being on medical leave. I recognized, more than ever, why so many people, including some of my friends, said they could no longer watch the news.

It was the shootings and killings, the house fires and carjackings, all the sickness and sadness and misfortune that they found so disturbing on the morning, afternoon and evening newscasts. Could that be what was affecting my decision? Or was it the guilt that I knew I would feel every time I reported on someone like myself, someone who had endured severe pain and reached the depths of despair yet *didn't* make it?

I sat watching the news that day in October 2005: a story of a six-year-old boy who had run into the street after hearing the music of an ice cream truck. He had been struck by a car and killed. "We have breaking news tonight," the news anchor said, "an incredible story in North Philadelphia . . ."

"No!" I screamed at the television. "It's an incredibly *tragic* story! It's an incredibly *sad* story! A little boy has died. A mother has lost her young son!"

The news anchor had told so many similar stories that

he had become numb to his most basic emotions. He no longer projected any feeling for human life. I didn't expect him to break down and cry, but I also didn't want to hear him tell me this story in the same way he would describe a city council meeting.

Night after night, it was one devastating and tragic story after another. They had become so commonplace that too many news anchors on TV stations, including my own, had lost their sense of compassion in presenting them. "God, please don't let that happen to me," I whispered to myself.

Physically, I was doing quite well. My voice was no longer thin and frail. In fact, it had improved significantly before my post-transplant visit to the Mayo Clinic in September 2004, and my persistent dedication to vocal therapy had brought dramatic improvement by the time I returned to Mayo for a biannual checkup in the spring of 2005. Also, my gastrointestinal issues had practically disappeared. My stomach was once again emptying properly, and my digestion was much better.

And I was no longer using a wheelchair. With my leg braces I could walk longer distances and stand for greater periods of time. Regular exercise in my pool had enhanced mobility in my feet, ankles and calves. I still had only very slight movement in my toes and persistent edema in my ankles, but my lower extremities were stronger and less rigid.

Thankfully, too, my hair was no longer a wreck. After falling out from the high-dose chemotherapy, it had first grown back a few inches, giving me a cute, close-cropped, curly 'do. Gradually, though, it grew to an awkward length, and the texture changed to unmanageably "nappy." I didn't want to chemically straighten it, but when my hairdresser used a flat iron on it, I looked like Moe from the Three Stooges. When the weather was humid, I looked like

Larry. But then, in the summer of 2005, I discovered hair extensions!

As for my mental state, I thought I was prepared to resume my reporter and news anchor duties. I had asked my local hematologist, Steve Cohen, to take me off Neurontin and Lyrica, which had been prescribed earlier for my polyneuropathy. Both medications had made me loopy and confused and had helped only minimally with the symptoms in my lower extremities.

What *was* helping my pain, I believed at the time, was the opioid pain medication OxyContin (generically called oxycodone). I was taking three 20-mg doses a day, and on some days, an extra pill. I didn't yet realize that I had developed a dependency on the narcotic. I would take my 20-mg pill, like clockwork, between 9:00 and 10:00 a.m., again between 5:00 and 6:00 p.m., then my last pill (plus, occasionally, one extra) before I went to bed, somewhere between 12 midnight and 2:00 a.m.

For me to return to Channel 6, Dr. Dispenzieri would have to give her consent, with a review by the ABC medical director. My biannual checkup with Dr. Dispenzieri in November 2005 went well, but she suggested I not return to work until the fall of 2006. She wanted my immune system to be stronger and my mobility to improve.

I listed my medications for her review, but not much was said about my OxyContin usage, only that if I wanted to taper off it in the future, she could give me some options.

RECOGNIZING
AN ADDICTION

Following my return from Rochester, Bill and I were out one Saturday evening, Christmas shopping, when I reached in my purse for my pill case. It wasn't there. I was almost an hour late taking the OxyContin. No worries, I thought, I'll just take it when we get home around 8:00. However, Bill noticed that I was becoming anxious and increasingly agitated.

"What's the dosage you're taking of that stuff?" he asked.

"20 mg. Why?" I responded.

"You were taking 10 mg twice a day. Now you're taking 20, two times a day? They're supposed to last 12 hours. Are you having more pain?"

"Obviously. Three times."

"Three times?" Bill asked.

"I'm taking it three times a day, have been for the past six months."

"That may be too much."

"I don't have any pain."

When we arrived home, I went straight upstairs for my pill case.

Bill suggested that the next time I saw my local doctor, I should talk to him about my OxyContin dosage and frequency. I promised I would, but never did.

About four months later, in March 2006, Bill and I were on our way with Leland to Philadelphia International Airport. It was spring break, and Lee's UVA roommate, Carlos Naupari, had invited him to his home in Rio de Janeiro for Carnival, a festival held every year before Lent in Rio. Lee would fly to Chicago, then on to Brazil, but we soon discovered that Lee, thinking his departure time was 5:30 p.m., had missed his actual 4:30 flight.

I was able to find another flight out of Dulles International, outside of Washington, DC. It would connect with a flight in Houston and get him to Rio within an hour of his initial arrival time.

The flight from Dulles was at 8:30 p.m. It was then about 4:35, and it would take us at least two and a half hours to drive from Philly to Virginia, but Bill and I thought we could make it. Lee was thrilled. There was only one drawback. I didn't have my 6:00 p.m. dose of OxyContin with me.

Remembering how I had felt when I was only about an hour late taking my medicine that Saturday before Christmas, I realized I would face one heck of a challenge. Bill assured me I would be fine, but I immediately began tallying the hours before we would be back home. I didn't really have a choice; we were already on our way.

For the next hour, I actually thought I *was* going to make the ride without any problems. But around 6:30 I felt a familiar twinge. I popped in a CD, *The Best of Cool Jazz*, hoping for a distraction. Lee and Bill were talking about UVA's football team. I drifted away in the music and my thoughts until 7:15. I was cold and shivering slightly. I had gotten in the back seat to allow my son and husband to enjoy their conversation and to keep them from focusing too much on me.

I curled up on the seat with a blanket covering me from feet to ears. I asked Bill if he had Benadryl or anything else to help me fall asleep. He didn't.

For what seemed like the next eight hours, I tossed and turned, sat up, lay down, hummed, counted expressway signs out the window, attempted to join my husband and son's conversation, cursed under my breath . . . then repeated it all.

When we finally arrived at Lee's terminal, I could hear Bill helping him with his bags and sending him off. I raised my head to try to say goodbye, but Lee beat me to it. He opened the back door to give me a crushing hug and sloppy kiss, promising to call after he got to Houston, before he boarded his flight to Rio. I was relieved for him, extremely nervous for me.

I thought about the long trip back to Philly and cringed, accidentally biting my lip. When Bill asked how I got blood there, I was too agitated to answer.

"Just get me home," I said. "Please!"

In my condition at the time, I was certain that Bill was intentionally trying to annoy me, but of course he was simply trying to deal with the situation. Still, in my mind, it was maddening that he could be so composed.

Before we left Dulles, I asked Bill if we might stop by a nearby hospital. As a physician, he might ask if I could get a shot of Valium or other sedative. Or perhaps he could write me a prescription for a syringe of Valium, and we could pick it up at a drugstore. He reminded me that he had medical licenses for Pennsylvania, New Jersey, New York and California, but not Virginia or Washington. I was going to have to tough it out.

That was the understatement of the year. By now I was even more jittery and enormously restless. On the way home, I counted to 100, forwards and backwards, recited nursery rhymes, and tried to sing with the songs on the radio; I tried to recount Lee's conversation, what I could remember of it—anything to divert my attention from how I was feeling. Bill would reach out to hold my hand; I would grab and hold tight, digging my fingernails in, then abruptly shove his hand away.

It had become obvious that I was no longer aware of my threshold for pain. I wasn't taking the OxyContin for pain. I was taking it because I *needed* it. I was dependent on it. I was addicted!

Once Bill and I arrived home, he brought my Oxy pill out to the car with a cup of water. I took it and didn't budge from where I was now gripping the back seat until the medicine began to take effect. I was already planning a call to Dr. Dispenzieri to ask her to enroll me in drug rehab.

By May the arrangements were made. I was going to return to Rochester to participate in the Mayo Clinic Prescription Drug Dependency program, enrolling in a two-week session after the Fourth of July and returning home for my 52nd birthday on July 19. With that plan in place, I became much more optimistic about rejoining the Action News team.

A FAMILY ADOPTION

There was also encouraging news from my brother, Tim, and his wife, Randi.

The adoption process in China had been dramatically delayed since December 2005 because of a huge scandal involving the kidnapping and selling of Chinese boys and girls to orphanages for profit. China began to require more extensive background checks on each child brought to an orphanage in the country. Officials checked reports of kidnapped children to see if they matched orphanage children. Officials also ran photos of the boys and girls on local news stations or in newspapers in every province to see whether anyone claimed those children.

China supposedly wanted to finish the trials for the kidnapping suspects before reopening the adoption program full-force. But Tim and Randi learned there would be no trials. The suspects were all executed in April 2006.

The next month, on May 25, Tim sent the following e-mail.

Lisa, JaNeen, Maria, Tom and Ted—meet your new niece! Lila Elise Howard! Just got this today!

Dear Tim and Randi,

Congratulations from all of us at La Vida International! We are happy to share the good news of your child assignment. Included with this message are scanned copies of the photographs that accompanied your child assignment information. . . .

Attached were three adorable photos of Lila, along with her birth name, Chang Yi Mei; her birthdate, 4/12/2005; her home province, Hunan; the name of her orphanage, Changde Social Welfare Institute; and other general health information.

GETTING HELP

I returned to Rochester, to take part in the prescription drug dependency program at St. Mary's Hospital campus at Mayo, soon after July 4, 2006. It was an outpatient program, just as my transplant had been, and I decided again to stay at the Holiday Inn by Marriott. I wouldn't need the connection to the Mayo Clinic buildings, but the hotel was extremely accommodating with its services, including grocery shopping and morning and evening shuttle service to and from St. Mary's. Neeny would again come to assist me for three or four days, as would my girlfriend Marsi Lattimore and my housekeeper, Anna.

And as it turned out, Tim and Randi were traveling to Beijing the same week to meet their new daughter. Tim created a blog so we could all follow their trip, and that proved to be a wonderful distraction from the work I needed to do to rid myself of the opioid that so clouded my thinking and suppressed my desire to return to work.

My schedule at St. Mary's began at 7:30 every morning. I would have a light, complimentary breakfast at the hotel, usually coffee and a muffin, and grab a banana or apple to eat during the 10-to-15-minute shuttle ride to St. Mary's. The program began with stretches from 8:30 to 9:30 a.m. Then we would have "Openers," a time to meet any new group members.

My group was a diverse gathering of young and old. There were 11 of us. I was the only African American. The youngest in our group was a 16-year-old girl from Madison, Wisconsin, who had broken her leg during a school soccer game and had developed a dependency on oxycodone, eventually abusing it during her recovery. There was also a mother of three, from the Twin Cities, who had become dependent on Percocet to help her get through her demanding day. It seems there's always a comic in the group, and ours was a tall 37-year-old farmer from Sioux City, Iowa, whom I'll call Bob.

"Whatcha in for?" asked Bob, as we began meeting and greeting each other.

"You make it sound like we're in prison," I replied. "I've been taking OxyContin."

"Oh man, me too. How much?" he asked.

"60 mg a day," I said. "Sometimes 80."

"Oh man, that's lightweight. Me, 120 mg, every day. You ever chew 'em?"

"No, never did."

"Too bad, you're missin' out on an all-time high. Try it next time," Bob suggested.

"I don't plan on there being a next time," I responded.

"Oh yeah? This is my fourth rehab," said Bob, almost bragging.

It turns out Bob had been to three drug addiction centers in his home state, but each time had gone back to using. His wife's uncle had been treated for cancer at the Mayo Clinic, and when she learned about its drug dependency programs, she gave him an ultimatum. "She told me she was giving me one more chance to get clean, or she was taking the kids and leavin'," he said with a shrug.

When we met our counselors and therapists, we found there was one of each for every four to five patients. This ensured that we all received the individualized attention and care that we were promised and needed. There was also a staff psychologist on site to supervise psychological testing, and a nurse to monitor those patients who self-administered their medications.

Like me, some patients in the group were participating in the program for two weeks, but most had enrolled for 30 days. It wasn't a surprise that Bob was with the 30-day team. Still, the 11 of us formed a small community and received 24/7 support in establishing our sobriety and developing recovery skills.

Our day consisted of lectures on everything from pain behaviors to personal relationships, relaxation techniques and weekend planning. The day also included two major PT (physical therapy) sessions, in which I really excelled. We also had OT (occupational therapy), and we experienced yoga and meditation as well.

The weather was beautiful during my stay in Rochester, and when it came time for me to be tapered off the OxyContin, my fears proved unfounded. The only side effects I developed were mild headaches and a few restless evenings with night sweats.

Meditation seemed to be most beneficial in my efforts to discontinue opioid use. I thought that perhaps I could have accomplished the goal on my own, but I gained a great deal by attending the program, namely a better knowledge of drug *and* alcohol abuse, addiction and recovery.

It was also a great arrangement for my caregivers because they could have most of the day to themselves, and then we would have time together in the early evening— to go to the mall, perhaps, or to have dinner at one of the many nice restaurants near the hotel. When JaNeen visited, she also attended "family day" one Friday, a day when patients' husbands, wives, children or other relatives come to the program to learn a little about it.

When my friend Marsi arrived to visit for a few days, we discovered the best salad I think I've ever had, at Victoria's Restaurant. It's an Asian-type salad with mangos, papaya, dried cherries, bean sprouts and a delicious sesame dressing. Both Marsi and I have tried to recreate it at home, but it was never quite as good.

My housekeeper, Anna, loved the time she spent with me. Not only was it an unexpected trip away from the humdrum of her regular schedule—cleaning, washing clothes and making beds at my house—but there was a Catholic church directly across the street from my hotel. She is a devout Catholic from Poland.

When I first hired Anna Kutyla, six years before my illness, she spoke very little English. I liked her personality and energy, and she had excellent references, but I told her then that I was concerned about our inability to communicate. She immediately produced a small handheld translator and informed me that she was committed to learning our language. Both of my boys, 13 and 10 at the time, promised to help her learn English. Also, I thought they could learn about her language and culture. Anna stayed with us for the next 14 years, and by the time of my drug treatment in Rochester, she was far more than a house-keeper to me.

⁓

As I mentioned, my brother's blog about the adoption trip to China was a welcome diversion during my program at St. Mary's. JaNeen and I tracked Tim and Randi as they visited the Great Wall of China and the Forbidden City, and when they flew to Hunan Province to meet Lila for the first time at her orphanage. She was the last of seven baby girls to be brought out, and she took to Tim immediately. He and Randi supposed that may have been because she had a male nanny caring for her at the orphanage.

Tim said Lila liked to grab his nose. On the street one day, he said, a pair of Chinese children began laughing and pointing at how tall Tim was and at his nose, which was much more prominent than theirs.

When the new parents brought Lila back to their hotel, she adjusted well, but Tim wrote in the blog that he and Randi noticed lumps on the back of her neck. The doctor who had evaluated all the babies had either failed to mention it or didn't think it significant. As it turned out, the lumps were Lila's lymph nodes, swollen from a recent skin rash. A doctor with their adoption agency, who came to the hotel to examine her, said they were probably the result of a heat rash, which was common in children at orphanages there. Tim was going to have a pediatrician examine her as soon as they got back to the States.

I reminded Tim that I would be leaving Rochester in two days, on my birthday, and exclaimed that I was opioid-free. He congratulated me, said they would be leaving China the following week, and promised we would meet Lila that weekend at my mom's house. I couldn't wait.

BACK HOME

It was unusually cold and foggy that morning as my school bus slowed to a stop and the kids from West Dunbar boarded. Sitting by the window in the middle of the bus, I just happened to glance outside to my right, and I noticed him. At least I thought it was him. I used the bottom edge of my sleeve to wipe away the condensation on the glass to get a better look. As I did, I heard murmurs and snickering surround me.

There, on the side of the two-lane highway, sitting in the frost-tipped grass and slumped against the chain-link fence in a thermal shirt and dirty jeans, was my dad. I hadn't known that he wasn't at home when I left the house. But I was well aware that he was on one of his binges, so I wasn't totally surprised.

At that moment I awoke, realizing I had drifted off to sleep on my family-room sofa. Unlike the terrifying dream about my brother Tom that had haunted me after college, this wasn't only a dream; it was a very real memory of an appalling and humiliating event in my childhood, one that reminded me how strong I was going to have to be in dealing with my health crisis.

The worst of my illness was over, at least for now. I had had a successful stem cell transplant and had kicked my prescription drug problem, but I had been away from work for more than two years.

As I thought about what I had been recalling in my sleep, I realized that living with my illness was going to be comparable, in some respects, to living with my alcoholic father. Because there was no intervention in my father's excessive drinking at an early age, he continued to have periods of prolonged drunkenness. Similarly, because my disease had not been diagnosed earlier, I had suffered some permanent nerve damage in my feet and lower legs. I probably would never be able to move my toes more than just slightly, and without regular therapy my ability to walk without leg braces would be compromised.

However, my penchant for remaining hopeful, and my desire to prove the experts wrong, had led to considerable progress. Less than six months following my transplant, I'd been able to stand on my toes, much to Dr. Dispenzieri's astonishment. And now she was giving me the okay to return to work, albeit part-time.

Still, I was anxious about it. I promised myself this would be just another hurdle to overcome.

CHAPTER ELEVEN

BACK ON THE JOB

I RETURNED TO WORK at Channel 6 a little more than five months after I completed the drug dependency program at Mayo. It was early January 2007, more than three years after I left. In the interim I had accepted sporadic assignments and appeared on various news segments in 2005 and 2006. I had even traveled to Chicago to report on Oprah's Legends Ball in 2005, and she in turn interviewed me about my illness. And I had taped several segments for our Thanksgiving Day parade in 2005 and 2006.

One thing I had promised myself all along: If I did regain my good health, I would remain an optimist, living life to the fullest. And I would continue to give back. I wasn't going to allow a rare disease to prevent me from preserving my career, from resuming my travels with my family, or from helping those less fortunate than myself.

A VACCINATION REBOOT

Returning to my old life did require some caution, though. My new local hematologist, Dr. Sameer Gupta (Dr. Cohen had retired and moved to Florida), told me to take it slowly, give myself time for my immune system to get strong again. And I knew it would be at least two years before I could travel abroad. With the transplant, my immune system had been totally wiped out and rebooted. I first had to renew all of my childhood vaccinations.

One year after my transplant, I received a Salk polio vaccine, along with shots for Hepatitis B, *Haemophilus influenzae* B and pneumonia (a pneumococcal 23-valent). I

My mom with me in 1995.

My mom with Leland in 1992.

Two of my favorite people at Channel 6: former sports anchor Scott Palmer (with his wife Kathy) and our late sports director, Gary Papa. His wife Kathy, a nurse, helped deliver Leland.

With Dave Roberts (far right) and other colleagues at the 6 ABC Thanksgiving Day Parade.

Bill and I joined Oprah, Patti LaBelle (far right) and her niece at a VIP reception following the premiere of *Beloved* in 1998.

Bill and I loved the Philadelphia Auto Show black-tie gala, sponsored by 6 ABC.

New Year's Eve, 2001:
six months later, I would
notice the first symptoms
of my mystery illness.

In Flushing Meadows, New York, at the U.S. Open Tennis Championship for
Langston's 18th birthday. Venus Williams can be seen in the background.

A year after my first bone marrow transplant, Leland and Langston gave me strength.

Wearing my curly "do"—with Leland in 2005.

Back on the job in 2006, I interviewed Oprah in Chicago for her 25th anniversary show. She also interviewed me about my illness.

With my sister-in-law, Neeny, hours after my second transplant was completed.

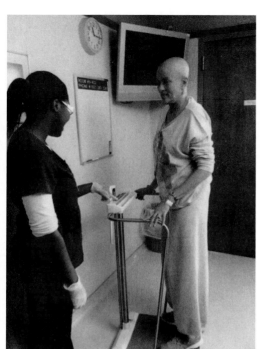

I put on a happy face for the nurses.

Back home enjoying dinner at Langston's apartment.

A bittersweet goodbye: with Jim Gardner and Adam Joseph on May 25, 2016.

After 38 years, I complete an old chapter and begin a new one.

also had a regular flu shot. All but the flu shot and pneumococcal vaccine were repeated in two months.

Two years after my transplant, I received a tetanus-diphtheria booster, another pneumococcal 23-valent, another Hep B and *Haemophilus influenzae* B, a third Salk polio vaccine, and the live vaccinations MMR (measles, mumps, rubella) and varicella zoster, the chicken pox vaccine.

In addition, I was told to get another flu shot and pneumococcal every year thereafter.

GIVING BACK

While I was ill, I had developed a strong desire to help African children. I had spent a lot of time watching television late at night when I couldn't sleep, and those commercials of children, sometimes playing in bare feet and ragged clothes around their grass huts, but most often starving, or even dying in their parents' arms, with an orbit of flies buzzing around their skeletal bodies, impelled me to act.

When you have worked nearly all your life and are suddenly unable to, you often feel unproductive. I needed to know that I still had a purpose in life beyond the people I loved, especially since my sons were becoming more self-sufficient every day. I needed to know that I could still make a difference, that in at least some small way I could help change someone's life.

After some research, I found two children to sponsor through World Vision, one of the oldest international child charities, dating back to 1950. It gets a top rating from charity watchdogs. I sponsored Kelechi, a five-year-old boy from Lesotho, and Fulami, an 11-year-old girl from Zimbabwe. What I liked most about World Vision was that I could get to know the children and follow their progress. My money would not only help them personally but assist their entire communities. I received letters regularly from both Fulami and Kelechi and from the organization.

In the first two weeks after I signed up, Fulami wrote to tell me that my support was helping her continue school even though she had become an orphan. She also told me that she was learning to improve her reading. Kelechi, with the help of his older brother, wrote to inform me that he too was going to school soon and that his family had purchased a new goat with part of the funds I sent. Both children sent photos of themselves and described their living conditions as well as their hopes and dreams. Both also told me the meanings of their names. Kelechi means *to glorify God*. Fulami means *one who demands respect*. The time I spent answering their letters lifted my spirts and filled me with a sense of pride.

Locally, I had joined Maternity Care Coalition, a nonprofit that operates in Philadelphia, Delaware and Montgomery counties in Pennsylvania. MCC's primary mission is to help underserved pregnant women and their children. It has assisted more than 40,000 mothers, teaching and empowering them to get better care for themselves during pregnancy, and helping them get a better start for their sons and daughters. Having been so sick myself, I realized how difficult it must be for those people who don't have the funds or other resources that I had been blessed with.

During my early involvement with MCC, I happened to meet an inspiring woman who had a son with big connections around the country and the world. Carolyn Smith had remained out of the limelight herself, but she told me she had been looking for a way to be of service to others in the city, to give back to the community where she had raised one of the most powerful actors in Hollywood. *His* name is Will Smith.

I introduced Carolyn to Maternity Care Coalition in the fall of 2007, and she went on to become one of its most loyal advocates and biggest supporters, co-chairing various events and fundraisers and making generous personal donations along the way.

A NEW JOB DESCRIPTION

After anchoring the news for nearly 30 years, I was reporting now, and filling in as an anchor for various newscasts, including the weekends. I had worried about how I would adjust to my new role, given my physical limitations. I had also worried about the deadlines I would face, but my colleagues were wonderfully accommodating.

Our assignment editor, Leslie Parker, would go out of her way to schedule my story later in the morning to give me more time to prepare, and in the first year she even made sure I was working with a photographer in a smaller news truck, one easier for me to climb into with my leg braces. One photographer, John Turner, when he knew he would be working with me, would even trade his news van for a smaller one.

All in all, it worked out much better than I had anticipated. I had come full circle. Reporting was how I had started in the news business, and it was what I loved most about my job.

In addition, my news director, Carla Carpenter, and general manager, Rebecca Campbell, agreed to allow me to cover mostly feature stories. My reports could be connected to hard news, but at this phase of my career I no longer wanted to cover murders, deadly fires and burglaries. I wanted to introduce our television viewers to more stories about people overcoming obstacles and illnesses in their own lives. I wanted to highlight the underdog and the surprising high achiever, like 19-year-old Kaheem Smith, a senior at Leap Academy Charter School in Camden. He was accepted to Cornell University, an Ivy League school, and highly rated Georgetown, despite the fact that he lacked a stable home life. And then there was the story of award-winning trombonist Jeff Bradshaw, who was preparing to record his third album live at the Kimmel Center. Bradshaw hailed from an impoverished section of Philadelphia, 12th and Poplar Streets, and he was bringing together some legendary recording artists, including Will Downing, Kenny Lattimore and Trombone Shorty.

I wanted our viewers to know that Peirce College had partnered with a unique program to combat unemployment in the city. I wanted to tell them about the elderly black man, Lewis Brown from the Mt. Airy section of Philadelphia, who at age 92 finally received his Doctor of Chiropractic diploma. I wanted them to see how Ather Sarif, a graduate student from Pakistan, a computer software engineer, paralyzed in a devastating car accident, wasn't giving up hope. Our viewers needed to see him receiving state-of-the-art treatment at Magee Rehabilitation Hospital in Philadelphia. They needed to know that he was planning to return to school, this time at the University of Pennsylvania.

I made sure our TV audience met Trish Shallenberger from Yardley, Pennsylvania, who took her Mary Kay skin care business to a whole new level after she met a 19-year-old Army soldier on a flight to Pennsylvania. She was headed home from a marketing convention; he was going to Fort Dix. Trish noticed his hands were red with huge blisters from his deployment in Iraq, so she gave the soldier some of her Mary Kay hand cream and promised to ship him and his unit more. After enlisting the help of her family and friends, and even her bible study group, she shipped

177 packages to Iraq less than four months later. Each was full of hand cream, lip balm, sunscreen, candy and notes from area school children. The soldier was shocked that she followed through on her promise and sent back a letter of gratitude. Months later, Trish sent an 800-package shipment to a battalion in Afghanistan. She was hoping that her once-small project would continue to spread love to soldiers and eventually become a registered charity.

And I was perhaps most eager to introduce our viewers to little Sarai Jackson of Egg Harbor Township, New Jersey, who suffers from alopecia universalis and has permanently lost all her hair. She and her grandmother, Johnice Lewis, came up with a unique idea to boost Sarai's confidence, to introduce her to the art of entrepreneurship and to help children with cancer and other diseases who also have lost their hair. It's called Kissy Face Kollections—colorful head wraps and hats with faux hair. Congressman Frank LoBiondo has cosponsored a Cranial Prosthetic bill that, if it becomes law, will have Medicaid pay for the products. Currently Johnice and Sarai donate the headpieces to ensure that every child with hair loss who wants one will get one. In addition, at age 10, Sarai will soon become an author! Like me, she is writing her first book, with the title *No Hair, Don't Care.*

GARY'S FIGHT ENDS

By early spring 2009, prostate cancer had taken a heavy toll on our sports director and dear friend Gary Papa. He managed to appear cheerful and hopeful on the air, but off-air we all saw just how difficult Gary's fight had become.

When he announced to our viewers that he was again undergoing chemotherapy and radiation treatments, many of us privately wondered if he could possibly emerge victorious this time. But no matter how bad a day Gary was having, working with him always produced a propitious environment for the rest of us. He offered his support when you least expected it.

One day during our five o'clock newscast, he slowly made his way to the sports chair next to mine at the anchor desk. I could see in my peripheral vision what a struggle it was for him, but I pretended not to notice when he threw up in the trash can at the end of the set. He slowly wiped his mouth, and when I finished reading my trio of stories and we headed to a commercial break, he said, "You know, it's like you never left."

"What, Gare?" I asked.

"You haven't missed a beat. You look as good as you did before you took medical leave."

"Thanks, Gare."

I couldn't help but see how ill *he* looked, which made what he said to me all the more special.

At that point, Gary often had to be helped from the sports office to the broadcast studio, and many of us would take turns giving him a ride home after a newscast. He worked until five weeks before we received word of his death on June 19. I got the call from Carla Carpenter that afternoon on my day off.

Our beloved colleague, who was so energetic, eager, erudite and often evasive about his own low ebb, had eventually descended into the unforgiving arms of cancer. But it was the mental and moral strength he displayed during it all that amazed us. I can't imagine that my friend truly didn't experience any genuine fear of death; surely he denied it, as I did. But how cruelly unfair it was that it crept upon him that Friday afternoon, snatching him from us at 2:57 p.m.

I sat in the big leather recliner in my family room that afternoon and was reminded of the vagaries of my own severe illness. As I watched the skittish black squirrels dart up and down and across the branches of the big ash trees above the wall in my back yard, I thought about what I would say on the air that night, during our televised tribute to Gary.

I recalled a letter I had received from a viewer more than three years earlier. I had saved it because of the comfort it brought me following my stem cell transplant and recovery. Surely, I would describe Gary's jaunty spirit; I would tell our viewers about how he would challenge me to race him on our way home following our *Monday Night Football* newscasts, usually well after midnight. But I would also share that letter, the one I had shared with him, the letter that had satisfied a question that both of us wanted answered: "Why us?"

"Why *not* us?" I had said once to Gary when we discussed the matter.

"But if you believe in God," Gary said," why would God let this happen? We're not bad people."

The woman who wrote me sent her message anonymously:

> Lisa, a decade ago, my daughter was very sick and dying. She was also in constant pain. I am a loyal Catholic, and my daughter's suffering made me question God. My little girl also had questions,
>
> "Mommy," she asked. "Why isn't God helping me get better? We have prayed to him, and we are a good family. Why isn't he answering us? Is he going to let me die?"

What the woman wrote next changed my religious perspective.

I could not tell my child that God has his reasons for sending her this terrible fate, or that God must have a special love for her to test her this way. So I told her that the God that I believe in did not send her this disease. Nor did he have a miraculous cure that he was withholding from her. But in a world in which we all possess immortal spirits in fragile and vulnerable bodies, God gives strength and courage to those who, unfairly and through no fault of their own, suffer pain and the fear of death.

Likewise, I could only tell Gary the same, and remind him of what that viewer had reminded me:

> . . . that he was more than a crippled body. He was more than someone with a debilitating illness. He was a human being with a loving family, with many, many friends, and with enough iron in his soul to remain a living person in the fullest sense of the word, until the very last day.

After I shared that letter during Gary's televised tribute, viewers called the station and wrote to ask for a copy of what I'd said. I have since learned that the latter passages are mostly an excerpt from the book *When Bad Things Happen to Good People* by Harold S. Kushner.

None of us knows why people die at the time and in the manner they do. I thought back to my first TV news partner in Philly, Jim O'Brien, and his sudden, tragic death more than two decades earlier.

We can attempt to understand it by envisioning what the world would look like if we all lived forever. On this subject, Kushner turns to a story from Jonathan Swift's classic *Gulliver's Travels*:

> In the land of the Luggnaggians, Swift writes in his fantasy, it happened once or twice in a generation that a child

was born with a circular red spot on its forehead, signify-
ing that it would never die. Gulliver imagines those children to be the most fortunate people imaginable, "being
born exempt from that universal calamity of human
nature," death. But as he comes to meet them, he real-
izes that they are in fact the most miserable and pitiable
of creatures. They grow old and feeble. Their friends and
contemporaries die off. . . . Their bodies contract various
ailments, they accumulate grudges and grievances, they
grow weary of the struggle of life, and they can never
look forward to being released from the pain of living.

More often than not, death becomes the only healer for
the pain we will eventually endure. Without it, humanity
would be deprived of a fresh start, as with the birth of a
child. Also, in a world where people live forever, we most
likely would have never been born.

However, it's one thing to explain that mortality is good
for humankind. It's quite another to try to tell someone
who has lost a child, or a parent, or a sibling, that death
is good. And it is quite something else to anticipate your
own death.

It is better, I think, that we acknowledge our vulnerabil-
ity to death as one of the existential conditions of life. We
can't explain it. We can't control it, or even always postpone it. All we can do is try to rise above the question "why
did it happen?" by asking ourselves, "What do I do now
that it has?"

⁓

The squirrels, so many of them, all black, continued their
daily ritual in my backyard: up and over, and back down. It
had become their normal protocol, their ceremonial after-

noon dance. Bill had said, jokingly, that they had migrated to our backyard because we were the only black family in the neighborhood. I remember looking for them in other yards during my power walks with Bobbi but never seeing any. One day I got up the nerve to ask Fran, a neighbor with whom I had become friends.

"Aren't they wonderful?" she said. "We have dozens of them."

I became almost hypnotized by the squirrels as I thought of Gary. These thoughts transported me back to *my* darkest hour and reminded me of the fragility of life. I would think of him and his wife, Kathy, his young sons, Tucker and Nathaniel, every day for months.

The last time he and I had had a long conversation was on our way home after one of our *Monday Night Football* newscasts. He had asked me simply and firmly, expecting nothing but an affirmative reply, "When you were the sickest, were you ever ready to die?"

"Yes, I was," I replied, remembering that although my response was truthful, and on one insufferable night I had even prayed to die, I never thought I would.

"I'm ready," he said.

Could it have been possible that he was ready to go, as he said? I would prefer, as we all did at the time, to remember him as the indestructible fighter. I had slipped him a note, months before: "If you ever need anything, please don't hesitate to let me know." It was just a gesture, but also a hope that someday, somehow, I *could* help.

He was one of those people in life who leave an immediate impression; mine of him was initially one of harmless raucousness. By the end, though, I saw him as a man of resolute purpose.

Gary became the face of the battle against prostate cancer in the Delaware Valley. He took his fight against the disease seriously, by the aggressive manner in which he fought it, by his dedication to the cause, and by never hesitating to allow his viewers to see him on air, even when he was undergoing chemotherapy and had lost weight and his hair.

As a tireless activist for prostate cancer awareness and research, Gary was honored by the city's Foundation for Breast and Prostate Health shortly after his death. The foundation's Father's Day run was named for him; the "Gary Papa Run 4 Your Life"—comprising 10K and 5K runs and 5K and 1-mile walks—takes place every Father's Day at the Philadelphia Museum of Art. June 18, 2017, marked the 15th year for the run, which saw dozens of Gary's former Channel 6 friends and colleagues participate.

CONNECTING WITH
OTHER PATIENTS

In August 2009 I returned to the Mayo Clinic for my biannual checkup with Dr. Dispenzieri. My pulmonary function had consistently improved since my 2004 transplant, and all of my other tests were good. At this point Dr. D asked me to take part in an international study on POEMS, and I was immediately willing. When I first visited her five years earlier, she and several other Mayo doctors were seeing about 300 patients from around the world with my syndrome. She was aware of about 115 POEMS patients who had undergone stem cell transplants. Those numbers had increased significantly over the last five years because more was known about the disorder, and many patients who previously had no diagnosis or the wrong diagnosis were now on the right track.

Dr. D told me she had recently diagnosed a rather young man from Mongolia with POEMS. His sister had contacted her, and she wondered if I would meet them to share my experience. Eagerly agreeing, I learned that the siblings were in Rochester and could meet me before I returned home the next afternoon.

I called the young woman from Mongolia, and we met that evening. The first thing I noticed was that she was sharply dressed. She had been educated in New York as an attorney, and had worked there for a few years before returning to East Asia to help the people there. She spoke nearly perfect English and was eager to know about my transplant, my outcome and my prognosis. Her brother, she told me, was in his early thirties. He owned a construction business in Mongolia, was very talented and smart, but had never left East Asia and spoke practically no English. She also explained that his illness had crushed his spirit; he had all but lost hope that he would get well again. She had taken him all over the world, she said, seeing many doctors about his sudden strange symptoms and weight loss. Even though Dr. D had given him a definite diagnosis and assured him he would make a major recovery, he was not optimistic. He was also embarrassed, she said, that he was now so frail and weak. She showed me a photo of him as a strong and muscular young man. I showed her photos of myself in a wheelchair, looking extremely ill, and she could see how much I had improved. However, she wasn't sure her brother would be willing to meet me. We agreed to try the next morning.

We met in the Mayo Atrium around 10:00 a.m. the next day. Her brother was still in their hotel room, she said, refusing to leave, so we chatted more about my journey with POEMS. Just before 11:00, she spotted him on the lobby escalator, heading toward us. I was stunned at how thin he was. He looked nothing like the pictures she had shown me of him. Still, I smiled, hoping to allay his fears, as he walked over and sat down beside me.

His sister spoke to him in his native language, and he solemnly nodded his head. She asked me to show him my photos of how I appeared several years earlier, and then demonstrate how I could walk now on my own. As I did, I saw a slight smile on his face. And then it came to me! I hurried back to the bench where I had been sitting and hastily took off my shoes and socks.

A wide grin now covered the young man's face, and he laughed out loud. His sister asked him to take off *his* shoes and socks, and surprisingly he obliged.

Our feet were almost identical. They were slightly discolored, both mine and his a pale blue with some swelling near the toes and ankles. And both his and my big toes overlapped the toes next to them. It had never been funny before, but now it was *hilarious*. And it was heartwarming because his sister and I knew that he got it: he knew that I had suffered as he was suffering, and then I had improved; I got healthy again. We knew that he was finally able to anticipate the same.

POEMS strikes first at the most distal points of the body, the toes and feet, sometimes the fingers and hands. It was my legs below my knees that had sustained some permanent nerve damage. POEMS had also struck the Mongolian man's feet first. So, even though we were at different stages in our diseases, my lower limbs would probably always resemble his.

However, his disease had not progressed as far as mine before his sister found Dr. D, who was now recommending he get radiation treatments. She didn't think he would need a transplant. He was the first person I had met who also had this rarest of illnesses, and we made a wonderful connection.

His sister and I stayed in touch by email for several years, long enough for me to learn that her brother, after being treated at the Mayo Clinic, had returned to his job as foreman of his construction company in Mongolia and was doing very well.

Since then, I have met and spoken with others suffering from POEMS, and I am confident that the contact has been therapeutic for all of us. I have also joined several patient forums, including Smart Patients, where POEMS sufferers and their caregivers share stories about living with the illness. I have found that some members of this online community are extremely knowledgeable about the disease. They are a powerful group, many of whom know much more about the syndrome than most doctors.

My current hematologist in Bryn Mawr, Dr. Sameer Gupta, is one of the few doctors who was already familiar with POEMS when I first experienced symptoms back in 2001. As a resident in India, Dr. Gupta worked on the research and data side of medicine; he remembers recording and reporting information on the stem cell transplants that were being performed on POEMS patients in India at that time. More than a decade and a half later, Dr. Gupta says the disorder can still be extraordinarily difficult to diagnose, especially early on: "Some of the criteria or symptoms will take weeks, months or even years to develop, and even though it is a hematological illness, it has autoimmune components."

Today, though, says Dr. Gupta, doctors are better at noticing and detecting the idiomatic signs of POEMS, and as more physicians become exposed to patients with the syndrome, and more information about the disease is disseminated, there will be more accurate and faster diagnoses: "Once you've had one patient with POEMS, then you'll begin testing other patients for the disorder."

A EUROPEAN GETAWAY

By late summer 2009, with Dr. Dispenzieri's consent, Bill and I decided to plan a trip to Italy for the fall. It would be a long-awaited trip for just the two of us.

I usually did all of our vacation planning, so with the help of a travel agent and my good friend, colleague and Philadelphia's favorite weatherman, Dave Roberts, born Dave Boreanaz, an expert on everything Italian, I decided on an itinerary of Venice, Florence and Rome. Bill made sure there was a good hospital near the hotels I chose in each city, just in case I had a problem, and we made the trip in October. It was a lovely getaway, just what we both needed.

My favorite city was Venice, because of the canals and gondolas and romantic atmosphere. The Piazza San Marco, Venice's most exquisite square; the Ca' d'Oro, the Golden House palace with its mosaics and beautiful architecture; and Murano Island on the Venetian Lagoon, famous for its beautiful hand-blown glass—all are sights I will treasure in my memory forever. Bill liked Rome best, for its history, monuments and museums. He loved visiting the Vatican, the Colosseum and the Pantheon.

We both agreed that Florence had the best food. You could get a pizza anywhere on the street, and it was better than any you had tasted before. And we quickly discovered that the local no-frills trattorias offered some of the most delicious cuisine in all of Italy. The fresh handmade pasta dishes at Sabatino's were inexpensive and just as tasty as anywhere you would go. Bill and I liked the places that were simple and Tuscan. The pastas were always perfect, and the meat dishes sublime. I liked the rabbit, while Bill favored the warm duck breast. And the wine! Every hole-in-the-wall osteria had a decent wine list.

A MUCH-NEEDED
FAMILY VACATION

Earlier in our marriage, when the boys were younger, we had always taken family vacations, most often to Disney World and the Caribbean, for the joys of exploration and fun in the sun. We had been to Disney World at least four times, once with my brother Tim and his son Alex. We had also taken the boys to Barbados, the Cayman Islands, Turks and Caicos, Anguilla and Saint Martin, Jamaica (Ocho Rios, Montego Bay and Negril) and Saint Lucia. They had enjoyed Montreal, Canada, which was usually a romantic getaway for me and Bill. We took Bebe on that trip with the boys, her first time out of the U.S.

As teenagers, they loved the family cruise we took with them at ages 13 and 11, when our ports-of-call were Puerto Vallarta (Mexico), Jamaica, Puerto Rico, the Dominican Republic and Labadee, Haiti. At the latter, I remember making it a point to take my sons from the beautiful private beach associated with the cruise lines into the nearby town to see first-hand the appalling poverty and the children begging on the streets for food and money. I hated it, but they needed to see that there were children and families who didn't live like them. Lang and Lee were stunned. They asked me if they could go back to the ship and bring the children of Labadee some of their clothes, or mail them some of their toys when they returned home.

My boys' absolute favorite, quick-to-get-to vacation spot is the Atlantis Paradise Island resort in the Bahamas. So it was no surprise that, in 2010, realizing that my long illness had postponed family vacations for the past six years, Leland asked to go to The Reef Atlantis hotel for his 25th birthday. It was one of Atlantis's newest and chicest hotel towers.

We arrived at Nassau Airport the week of Lee's birthday on August 9. Once we made our way to the Atlantis, Lang and Lee were thrilled to learn that Bill and I had decided against the two-bedroom suite we had originally planned and instead had gotten them their own suite with double beds, on the same floor as ours. After all, they were men now. The only thing we insisted that they *not* do, as men, was purchase weed from the locals across the bridge in Nassau.

The second afternoon we were there, Lee came pounding on our door, bursting with excitement. He was so ecstatic we could barely understand him, but what we did decipher was that the Miss Universe pageant contestants were staying at the Atlantis.

Before Lee's exuberance finally wore him out, we also discerned that the contestants were hosting a VIP party at the adjacent Cove Atlantis tower in two nights. Before Bill could ask, Lee assured us that, yes, he and his brother *would* get tickets.

True to their promise, the pair managed to secure four VIP tickets to the big event, and we all set out to a meet and mingle with nearly 50 of the most beautiful and talented girls in the world. We could hear the reggae music as soon as we stepped out of our hotel. And Bill was as giddy as his sons.

"Miss Venezuela, here I come," he bellowed as we walked around the pool deck to the Cove patio entrance.

"Get a grip," I hollered back. "Don't embarrass me."

Once inside the party, we were surprised to see that

there were few restrictions on the contestants. There were guards around the premises, but guests were chatting up the girls and dancing with them. Lee and Lang wasted no time getting in on the action.

I became the designated photographer as the Laury men posed with one beauty after another, Lee with Miss Costa Rica, Miss Romania and Guatemala, and Lee again with Miss Albania, Miss Kosovo and Miss Peru. There was Lang cozied up with Miss Colombia and Miss Cayman Islands, and then with Miss Aruba. I couldn't tell who the other contestant was, Lang was holding her so close.

I hadn't seen Bill and Miss Venezuela yet, but there he was with Miss Brazil and Miss Bulgaria.

Wouldn't you know, it was Lee who connected first with Miss Venezuela, who I learned had won Miss Universe the previous year and was a favorite again that year. (Weeks later, as we watched the pageant at home, Miss Venezuela took the top prize again.)

There were Misses Finland, Iceland and Ireland, sitting by themselves. Not for long I was sure. And Miss Bolivia asked *me* to take a photo together. Surprisingly, she was taller than me—and not so surprisingly, much thinner.

After filling a plate with pork, conch fritters, jerk chicken and island rice at the buffet, Bill finally caught up with Miss Venezuela, but he appeared to be really fond of Miss Curaçao. By now Lang was in a deep conversation with Miss Guyana, who was adorable, and so were Miss Zambia and Miss Jamaica. Bill thought Miss Bahamas, too, was a stunner.

One of the girls got so drunk, I was told, a guard had to escort her to her room when she began to dance provocatively. No titles, but it rhymed with "mice men."

Needless to say, we had a blast!

CHAPTER TWELVE

DISAPPOINTING
NEWS FROM
MAYO

In April 2012 I was back at the Mayo Clinic for an annual checkup. It was nearly eight years since my bone marrow transplant, and I was feeling pretty darn good.

I knew there was no cure for POEMS, which had permanently damaged the nerves in my feet and legs and temporarily impaired other parts of my body; my doctors had called it a "smoldering myeloma." Yet as I sat in Dr. Angela Dispenzieri's office waiting for her that cool spring afternoon, I was worried about only one thing: that she would tell me I had diabetes. During my visit the year before, she had stunned me by announcing I was borderline diabetic. About two-thirds of all patients with POEMS syndrome will develop diabetes mellitus. My weight had risen to 174 pounds, which wasn't that bad for my 5 foot 9½ inch frame, but I had a sweet tooth and a love of carbs, which would heighten my propensity for developing the disease. By now I had cut back but still had a tendency to overindulge in sugary drinks and pasta. And my paternal grandmother had been diabetic.

MORE POEMS

When Dr. Dispenzieri entered, she immediately announced that she had good news and bad news, and I instantly assumed the bad news was diabetes.

"No, your blood sugar numbers are much improved," she said.

"Then what on earth?" I asked.

"Your light chains are reaccumulating . . . it's the IGA . . . and your platelets, they're not anywhere near out of control,

148

but they're on the rise . . . and we want to be proactive. Nip this thing in the bud early."

The bottom line: My illness, POEMS syndrome, was rearing its ugly head again. I was crushed.

Dr. Dispenzieri gave me a short list of possible options, but recommended I start by taking a chemotherapy pill called Revlimid. It is commonly used to treat anemia, a lack of red blood cells in the body, as well as multiple myeloma, a cancer resulting from a progressive blood disease (my disease, POEMS, was its cousin) and mantle cell lymphoma, a rare cancer of the lymph nodes.

Revlimid is also used in patients with myelodysplastic syndrome, or MDS, caused by an abnormal chromosome, a disorder suffered by *Good Morning America*'s Robin Roberts, who had a bone marrow transplant in 2012. Our illnesses are similar but involve different clones of abnormal cells. In Robin and other people with MDS, the bone marrow doesn't produce enough healthy blood cells. In people like me with POEMS syndrome, there is an overproduction and often improper function of plasma cells in the bone marrow. This often results in the formation of sclerotic bone lesions and an overabundance of M proteins in the blood.

Robin's sister was the perfect match and was able to donate her bone marrow to Robin. In my case, remember, my stem cell transplant was autologous, meaning I was my own donor. The bone marrow not used in my 2004 transplant had been frozen and stored for use in any future transplants I might need. I had been convinced, however, that it would never *be* needed. In fact, I had envisioned those cells sitting in trays in the Mayo freezer for so long they'd develop freezer burn, or perhaps, when the doctors realized I would not be needing them, they would use them for someone else's life-saving transplant.

I didn't want to think about the news from Dr. Dispenzieri. I couldn't be going through this again. How could I? I had improved tremendously. Yes, I had some permanent nerve damage, but I'd been able to ditch the wheelchair and, recently, even the leg braces. Yes, I had been told that I might one day need another stem cell transplant, but I had expected to *feel* sick again first.

I thought about my journey so far, from my first illness and transplant. There had been endless hurdles. But that was what I had come to know about life from a young age. There were always hurdles. You just had to make your way over them.

TRANSPLANT #2

My hematologist in Bryn Mawr, Dr. Gupta, worked in conjunction with Dr. Dispenzieri at Mayo. After I experienced some gastrointestinal side effects with the Revlimid, he suggested I try a chemo medication called Velcade. However, after about a year, we realized that while it was preventing the progression of my illness, Velcade wasn't improving my condition.

In 2013 Dr. D suggested that I return to Mayo to have more of my "good" marrow harvested in preparation for a probable second bone marrow transplant. She wanted me to have more, newer cells to supplement those already in storage. I knew it would be difficult for Bill to go with me; it was his busiest time of the year. My dear friends Marie Henderson and Pat Williams, a doctor herself, came instead, at the end of the week, and helped make it a fun time.

Thankfully, I completed most of the stem cell harvesting before Ree and Pat arrived, because the process involved some complications. As with my first bone marrow harvesting, doctors planned to retrieve the marrow from my circulating blood, not my actual bone marrow. Normally this is a fairly simple process. However, I wasn't producing enough stem cells, so I was given injections of a growth factor drug into my stomach, a drug that stimulates the growth of stem cells in the marrow and releases them into the bloodstream. I had the growth factor injections for four days, suffering side effects of fever, chills and muscle pain, before doctors were able to collect enough stem cells for use in my next transplant.

After all that preparation, the harvesting process itself took only about three and a half hours. As before, a catheter was placed in a large vein in one of my arms, and my blood flowed through the catheter to a special cell-separating machine that separated and collected the stem cells. The process is called apheresis. The stem cells were then frozen and stored.

Pat and Marie arrived in time to sit with me through my last harvesting session, and that night all we wanted to do was order some dinner, relax in the hotel and maybe watch a movie. As it turned out, the HBO political drama *Game Change*, about the 2008 presidential campaign of John McCain and Sarah Palin, was one of the movie selections on our hotel TV. Marie and I had seen it; Pat had not, but had heard what a tauntingly terrific job Julianne Moore had done portraying Palin. We laughed and ate and talked long into the night about the Alaskan governor and her ill-fated attempt to win the vice presidency. And I forgot all about those irksome needles in my belly.

HERE WE GO AGAIN

I procrastinated for the next year and a half. For one thing, I didn't feel that sick. It was only the chemo pill that made me feel less than 100%. Also, I had a difficult time succumbing to the inevitable and leaving work again, knowing that this time I would probably not return. I was both excited and a little nervous about starting a new life journey.

But in early April 2015, I was back at Mayo for my second transplant. I knew the drill and was eager for it all to be over.

It was another two months in Rochester. Neeny, Marie and Pat split up the caregiver duties, along with Langston and Leland. They all helped make my transplant trek more tolerable. The only unexpected episode occurred when the nurses informed me I would be receiving double the dose of chemo I had gotten during my first transplant. They reminded me that I had been too sick to receive the full dose in 2004. For nearly two weeks, that heavy dose caused so many painful ulcers in my mouth that I couldn't swallow. However, I was fine sucking banana popsicles and cherry Jello until my mouth sores disappeared.

On the third or fourth day of my chemo, when my hair began shedding on my pillow, Langston shaved my head. Once my appetite returned, Lee fixed me the best pancakes, bacon and scrambled eggs.

The following year, in May 2016, I officially retired. WPVI threw me a big bash at the station. Before the party, accompanied by colleagues Jim Gardner, Adam Joseph and Ducis Rodgers, I said an emotional goodbye on set to all of our wonderfully loyal viewers.

Two months later, on July 28, three days before her 86th birthday, our dear Bebe quietly passed away. It truly was going to be a new and unfamiliar chapter in my life.

CHAPTER THIRTEEN

LIVING WITH
A CHRONIC
ILLNESS

I WRITE THIS final chapter of my book as I approach age 63. Sometimes I feel as though I'm 25. More often, my feet and legs mimic those of a 90-year-old. My life now is different than I thought it would be. I am not as fast, as active or as pain-free as I had hoped. Still, I am relishing a challenging, yet blessed life.

Yes, I've been able to purchase things I never thought I would own. Travel to places I couldn't imagine I'd ever see. But have I been successful? I'm still working at it. I've learned that it really does depend on how you define success.

Former *Essence* magazine editor-in-chief Susan Taylor shared this in one of her columns more than 25 years ago, and I still try to live by it today.

> Most people define success in material terms . . . but when you think about it, success is how you come to understand yourself and the world you live in; it's how you define your needs and goals in life; how you define and deal with your problems; how you handle the everyday stresses and strains of your life. Success is also learning to forgive yourself [for me, it's forgiveness for my impatience, my past aggressions and unintended slights], because an apology isn't really worth much unless you're able to forgive yourself. I'm learning to be successful in my soul. When you really think about it, success is feeling good about yourself. It's liking. . . . And loving yourself, and that love must be internalized.

Nor have I forgotten these words of hers:

Each of us has a right to a happiness that transcends all
the materialistic forces that surround us. Each of us has a
right to a joy that we nurture and sustain from the well-
spring of our beings. But it is a commitment as a human
being first. You can't give love until you have love to give
and you only have love to give when you love yourself.

Leland also expressed what he learned from my illness:

Over time I realized that the answers to all my timorous
questions weren't as important as I once thought. What
really matters is that I still get to talk with my best friend
every day—my mom is still here. Sure, we have our dis-
agreements here and there, but they are almost as fun
as our laughs. I have to admit—I still enjoy pushing her
buttons—it's all done out of love. More than anything
else, my mom's illness has taught me to never take for
granted how much she means to me. I can honestly say,
"if she's not okay, I'm not okay." I am forever grateful for
every moment we spend together.

When I think of my childhood these days, it is full of
happy memories: summer afternoons with my brothers,
snacking and playing on a blanket under our apple tree . . .
Christmas mornings, ripping open presents amid squeals
of excitement . . . the smell of grits and sausage on the old
white stove in our kitchen . . . Easter egg hunts in frilly
dresses and bonnets, my brothers in short suit-pants and
ties. And drive-in movies in our PJs, curled up in sleeping
bags in the back of our station wagon.

But the innocence and merriment of childhood are
fleeting. Life changes and isn't always fair. Still, I have

those wonderful memories, memories only a mother could shape. I think of my mother often, wishing I had known her better and longer. I don't cry now when I see her face in photos or videos, or even in my mind when I'm alone. I am no longer grieving her loss; rather, I'm rejoicing in the memories—and in the lessons she left me and all of those who loved her.

I thank my mom for so many things, even for my strict Catholic upbringing, because, though I no longer follow Catholicism, it instilled in me a sense of spirituality. It has given me the faith that I am connected to something greater than myself; a sense that there is order in the universe—a higher power, or a center within me from which my strength springs. It doesn't matter whether I know him or her or it as God or Allah or Buddha. What's important is the assurance that I'm not all alone.

I thank my dad, also; his presence in my life when I was young was a great solace to me. For so many years I asked myself how I would reconcile my ideal of the perfect, doting father with the reality of the unacceptably flawed man he became, a man I couldn't understand. Finally I realized that the answer was simple. I have forgiven him. And I am comforted by the knowledge that he loved well, when he was able. Like me, he suffered from a disease.

His disease limited him emotionally. But when I am lost in reverie, I sometimes imagine what he might say to me today: "Not bad for a little yellow colored girl from Institute."

I shake my head at his silliness, then remember how fortunate I've been to have experienced misfortune in my life. I've gained much more knowledge in my pain than I have in my bliss, and I appreciate my happiness more, having understood sorrow.

ACKNOWLEDGMENTS

I have known for a long time that I would eventually write this book. In 2003, when it became all too clear that I wasn't going to get a quick answer to what was causing my baffling illness, I began taking notes and keeping a journal of my experiences. I thank my mom and my husband, Bill, for encouraging me to do so.

I offer my heartfelt thanks to two doctors at Main Line Health, Dr. Steve Cohen and especially Dr. Gary Newman, who consistently suggested that I visit the Mayo Clinic for another opinion on my disease. Gary went above and beyond. He cared, and he ultimately led me to the person who made all the difference in my recovery, Dr. Angela Dispenzieri at Mayo. Thank you, Dr. Dispenzieri, for your hard work and research on this rarest of illnesses; thank you for saving my life!

My stem cell transplant teams, both in 2004 and in 2015, were the best of the best. The members of the transplant nursing staff at Mayo Clinic are adroit professionals who demonstrate compassion and empathy for patients in their care.

I knew our Channel 6 viewers were special, too, but they exhibited something more when I returned to work following my first transplant. When I was reporting in one of Philly's many neighborhoods, not a day went by that someone didn't say that she or he prayed for me while I was away from work. I am a huge believer in the power of prayer, and I am confident that all of those prayers said for me played a huge role, first, in my finding the right doctor to accurately diagnose and treat my disorder, and later in my healing.

I kept my desire to share my journey with others in the back of my mind for nearly 12 years, occasionally writing a paragraph or a partial chapter here and there. Before my retirement, advertising and public relations executive Brian Tierney, a family friend, suggested I get serious about the book. A shout-out to Brian, and to Nina Zucker as well. After my retirement in 2016, Nina, who had written our Thanksgiving parade scripts at Channel 6 and now has her own PR company, introduced me to her childhood friend Gloria Hochman. What a godsend! Gloria, an award-winning author and journalist who still writes for the *Philadelphia Inquirer*, offered me invaluable guidance, support and assistance in the very early stages of my manuscript. Thank you, Gloria!

I again thank Bill and my sons, Leland and Langston, who never let up when I had my doubts about the book project: "Mom! When are you going to write your book? You can help so many people!" And that's what inspired me the most: the possibility of helping someone, in some small way, by sharing my journey openly and honestly.

Finally, thank you, God, for allowing me to be a conduit through which your message of hope and faith has flowed.

A NOTE ON RESOURCES

A lot has happened in medicine since I had my first bone marrow transplant in 2004. More doctors are familiar with POEMS syndrome, and a number of advanced bone and stem cell transplant programs are now available in Pennsylvania. In Philadelphia, Jefferson Health offers the Blood and Marrow Transplant Program at the Sidney Kimmel Cancer Center. Penn Medicine has the Abramson Cancer Center's Bone Marrow and Stem Cell Transplant Program. Fox Chase–Temple University Hospital has a Bone Marrow Transplant Program centered at Jeanes Hospital. In Pittsburgh, the Hillman Cancer Center of the University of Pittsburgh Medical Center (UPMC) is one of the largest providers of stem cell transplant services in the state.

I would be remiss if I didn't share with you important information about Be the Match, the largest and most diverse marrow registry in the world. Operated by the National Marrow Donor Program, its mission is to save lives through cellular therapy. Please go to https://join.bethematch.org to see how you can save a life by becoming a marrow donor.

ABOUT THE AUTHOR

LISA THOMAS-LAURY is a retired news anchor in Philadelphia.

She began working at WPVI-TV, Channel 6, the city's ABC affiliate, as a reporter and co-anchor of Action News in 1978, at the age of 24. She covered the stories of everyday people around the region, as well as numerous political elections and conventions and the activities of political figures, from Massachusetts Senator Ted Kennedy to President Ronald Reagan and the inauguration of President Bill Clinton.

In 1981 she received high praise for her reports from London on Prince Charles and Lady Diana's wedding. However, the stories she loves to tell the most are those of average people with unique experiences, and those who overcome major obstacles in their lives.

In 2001 Lisa began facing her own significant life challenge. She was struck with a rare nerve disorder that remained misdiagnosed for nearly two years. She left WPVI temporarily when her disease paralyzed one of her vocal cords. Lisa underwent a bone marrow transplant at the Mayo Clinic in Rochester, Minnesota, in 2004 and returned to Channel 6 two and a half years later.

Lisa has received three honorary doctorate degrees and numerous other awards, including an Emmy for a public affairs documentary on Philadelphia neighborhoods in the 1980s and the city's most prestigious accolade, the Liberty Bell Award. She retired in May 2016 after a second bone marrow transplant, having spent nearly four decades with WPVI-TV.

12/17